MORE
STORIES OF
INSPIRATION

NASPA
Student Affairs Administrators
in Higher Education

MORE
STORIES OF
INSPIRATION

51 Uplifting Tales of Courage, Humor,

Healing, and Learning in Student Affairs

SARAH M. MARSHALL
EDITOR

NASPA
Student Affairs Administrators
in Higher Education

More Stories of Inspiration: 51 Uplifting Tales of Courage, Humor, Healing, and Learning in Student Affairs

Published by NASPA – Student Affairs Administrators in Higher Education
1875 Connecticut Ave., NW
Suite 418
Washington, D.C. 20009

Additional copies may be purchased by contacting the NASPA publications department at 301-638-1749 or visiting http://bookstore.naspa.org.

Library of Congress Control Number: 2009928549

ISBN 978-0-931654-15-2

Printed and bound in the United States of America.
FIRST EDITION

CONTENTS

Introduction

I am honored to coordinate this second volume of *Stories of Inspiration*. The response to the first book has been powerful. I have heard accounts of readers feeling validated as a result of reading the motivational realities from the first volume. I even had one vice president tell me that she gave the book to her president so that he could "finally" understand the role of student affairs on campus and in the lives of students. I think the success of the first volume was because readers felt a connection with the stories. Through the stories, they found professional meaning and purpose.

I am delighted to share with you this second volume and hope that it, too, touches you in some way. As I stated in the earlier book, I believe student affairs is a heroic profession. We give of ourselves to help others. Despite the challenges of declining budgets, changing student populations, and troubling economic times, our work remains significant. We impact the future via our students. Given the reality of today's challenges, finding the inspiration to continue to aid students and their parents is possibly more difficult than ever. The timing of this book is significant because positive reinforcements in student affairs can be few and far between. The authors of these stories share their precious meaningful and humorous moments with you.

Stories were collected over the course of six months from student affairs educators of all levels, from undergraduate students to vice presidents. This collection of stories draws on a variety of emotions. Some inspire, motivate, and rejuvenate, while others provide comic relief. These stories allow us to learn through the experiences of others and challenge us to identify lessons that may improve our practice. They help student affairs professionals find purpose in what we do, reinforce the significant role we play on college campuses, teach us valuable lessons, or simply help us laugh.

SOLICITATION AND SELECTION OF STORIES

Stories for this book were solicited in a variety of ways. A call for stories detailing the purpose and submission criteria for the book was distributed. The call was posted on the NASPA website, included in NASPA weekly e-mail updates, and circulated on many professional list-servs. The call was also sent to program faculty, senior student affairs officers, and NASPA regional vice presidents who were asked to share the submission criteria with their various constituents.

In total, 110 stories were submitted for consideration. Each story was reviewed by three evaluators. Stories were evaluated for clarity of purpose, their touching/humorous nature, overall significance to student affairs, and the quality of writing. Included in this volume are the personal accounts of 48 individuals telling 51 stories. Selections were based on reviewers' feedback and the uniqueness of the story. Every effort was used to attain a diverse group of storytellers in terms of gender, race, number of years in the profession, institutional type, and division of student affairs. While taking these characteristics into consideration, the ultimate goal was to find the most interesting and moving stories.

ORGANIZATION OF THE BOOK

This volume is organized similarly to the first. Read it at your leisure or all in one setting. You can start with the first story and end with the last, or reverse and start at the end. You can randomly read one story at a time. Each narrative has its own unique message. As learned in the review process, different stories touch people in different ways. You may be particularly moved by one story, while a colleague prefers another.

This book is intended to rejuvenate those who have been in the field for some time as well as inspire others who are early in their careers. Ideally, it provides a positive, inspirational, and even humorous look at the profession while reinforcing the significance of student affairs work.

Sarah M. Marshall
May 11, 2009
Mt. Pleasant, MI

More Than Just 20%

Anne Ehrlich

Those of us who have spent more than a few years working with student governments, resident advisors, and programming boards are familiar with the old "80/20" adage—that 80% of the leadership positions on campus are held by 20% of the students. I know I speak for all of us when I say we love those students! We love their dedication, their commitment to campus life, the time they spend hanging out in our offices, and their visible enthusiasm as they realize they have made a difference in the lives of those around them. Much of the vibrancy on our campuses exists thanks to this devoted 20%.

Angie was not part of that number. She never held a campus leadership position and, as far as I know, she never set foot in the student affairs suite. In fact, the first time I ever saw Angie was when I was sitting in her family's kitchen watching the news coverage of her death. A photo of this 19-year-old who had just been killed in a senseless car accident flashed across the TV screen. Her smile lit up the room.

The next day, as my colleagues and I set about the heart-wrenching task of notifying our campus community of her death and planning a memorial service, I was apprehensive. I wanted to do that smile justice. I wanted to be able to talk about Angie and what our community had lost by losing her. But, at that point, I have to admit I didn't exactly know what that was. She wasn't part of the 20%. She wasn't a student I knew particularly well. Okay, she wasn't a student I knew at all.

But others certainly did. The very first faculty member I talked with asked if he could join us as we visited the rest of Angie's classes. He had been so taken by Angie's unwavering smile (even in the face of grueling accounting exams) that he wanted to do something to pay tribute to her. As we spoke with more and more faculty, staff, and students, we discovered that others felt much the same way. One classmate commented on Angie's amazing ability to get a group that seemed doomed from the start to work together seamlessly on a class project. In a management class, a student smiled as he told us how Angie could always cheer people up with her jokes—not because the punch lines were particularly funny, but because she would undoubtedly dissolve into fits of laughter before she was halfway done. Another professor commented on how Angie's area of concentration—human resources—seemed so appropriate because she had an uncanny knack for finding the good in everyone—and inspiring others to do the same. The stories went on and on.

By the time I sat down to write out my remarks for Angie's memorial, I had plenty to say about what lay behind that smile. During the service, which felt like a celebration, faculty, staff, and students came forward to share the lessons Angie had taught them. I reflected on how this young woman quietly yet strikingly affected those around her, and I realized that maybe that 20% was really a much larger number than I had originally thought.

Today, my colleagues and I still have plenty to say about Angie. We talk about her to incoming students during orientation. We show them a picture of Angie and her smile and tell them her story. And we tell them—as Angie reminds us—that each and every one of them has the potential to inspire our community, whether they aspire to be part of the 20% or not.

My Name Is Vivian

Carol A. Lundberg

D igging through my e-mail inbox, I regularly discover student e-mail addresses that reveal an identity different from what they bring to my classroom. I have seen things like dumbblond@...com or surfer-dude@...net, but in my recent search for an e-mail from Vivian, I noted that the name on her university e-mail account was Hsin-Yi. I thought of Jennifer, whose real name was Chien-Yu, and of Rachel, whose Chinese name I didn't know. I had been happy to accept these names, though I knew they were not the names their parents had chosen, the names that honored a relative or reflected a value of their family. Rachel explained to me that since her name would be difficult for Americans to pronounce, she chose an easier one. What does it mean to change one's name, even if informally, for the sake of a person who might be unwilling to put in the effort to learn the real name? What does it say about me when I readily use the new name without questioning the need for its creation?

This happens not only with Chinese names, but with many others. I drop the tilde on the "n" in my friend Nancy Quiñones' last name when I write it. Surely I could be doing something more important with that split second it takes to get her name right.

Variations on names are often accepted, especially by people who don't occupy the dominant space in an organization. I'm reminded of a student named Mireya, who was often called Maria. I overheard her explain to a busy faculty member that she was okay with either name, realizing that her name was difficult. My own name, Carol, also has variations. People sometimes call me "Carolyn" or "Karen," but I always correct them, not giving it much thought. That luxury is not afforded to Mireya, Hsin-Yi, or Rachel; they have given it quite a bit of thought. Their alternative names are just one of many accommodations they make to negotiate their way in a college or university where they often feel like outsiders.

Laura Rendón's model of validation[1] speaks of boosting minority student success by explicitly valuing them—affirming their identity, culture, values, and beliefs as important elements of the university. She argues that such validation is a precursor to their involvement in the college experience and to their full benefit in terms of learning. Sheepishly, I realize it is not terribly validating for me to call a student "Vivian" when the people who really know her use Hsin-Yi.

As I reflect on students who have changed their names for my sake, I wonder what else they have changed, other aspects of them that I have readily overlooked because it was easier than paying attention. Hsin-Yi came to my house for dinner the other night, and I served Sloppy Joes. Her interest in the odd name and the history of this dish (if Sloppy Joes can be considered a dish) revealed her sincere interest in my background. Her approach was educational for me. It taught me to slow down and pay attention, not only to her name, but to who she is. Sloppy Joes are not central to my identity, but her interest showed me that she cared, that she wanted to know about me. Indeed, I felt validated.

---

1   Rendón, L. I. (1994). Validating culturally diverse students: Toward a new model of learning and student development. *Innovative Higher Education, 19*(1), 33–51.

FALLING FOR YOU: HUBRIS
AND THE NEW PROFESSIONAL

KRISTEN A. RENN

E veryone has a past: every senior student affairs officer, every dean, director, and tenured faculty member in student affairs. Hopefully, our past can help us be better educators. An incident from my past helps me remember—20 years later—what it's like to be a new professional in student affairs and how not to take myself too seriously.

I started my career in student activities and student unions. As assistant director of student activities, I was responsible for the Union Activities Board's (UAB's) annual Spring Weekend. On a campus dominated by radical politics, protests, and postmodernism, Spring Weekend was a nod to stereotypic college life: rock bands, fraternity parties, too much alcohol. As advisor to UAB, I spent much of the weekend supporting student leaders behind the scenes, dealing with demanding performers and their grumpy agents, working with my colleagues on the campus police force to deal with indoor events that exceeded the fire limit, and placating senior administrators who lamented the annual bacchanal.

During my first year, the academic calendar was such that Spring Weekend—traditionally held just before the reading period for final exams—coincided with visiting days for newly admitted students and, at the last minute, a congressional hearing to be held at the university. After campus neighbors complained about R-rated public behavior on previous Spring Weekends, the mayor promised that this year a local ordinance forbidding public nudity would be enforced. Campus feminists planned to protest discriminatory policies that allowed men to go shirtless but insisted that women's bodies be covered. It was the perfect storm on the main green. To the west, fraternity brothers staged Trikes for Tykes, a fundraising event, ostensibly alcohol-free, that featured teams of inebriated students on tricycles. To the east, about a hundred topless students, male and female, sunned themselves in defiance of the mayor. From the south came campus tour guides, followed by dozens of eager parents towing their nonchalant, newly admitted offspring. From the administration building, the university president, his cabinet, several congressional representatives, and a gaggle of news cameras awaited.

I was in my office, overlooking the green, when the phone rang. The dean of students wanted me, as a woman, to confront the topless students on the green. The institution was embroiled in an ugly, public debate about how best to handle cases of alleged sexual harassment and sexual misconduct against students. The dean and several staff members were accused of insensitivity toward women. It was not the time for him or any of his male staff to attempt to negotiate with bare-breasted women, in full view of the national media. Several of the student protesters were identified, at a distance, as members of the (then) Lesbian, Gay, and Bisexual Alliance (LGBA). I was the dean's liaison to this community. Perhaps I had some special power of influence that could get these students to put their shirts on, the dean suggested.

Although I had what I considered more important tasks to accomplish related to the larger dimensions of Spring Weekend, I told the dean I would try. My plan was to go out, ask the students to put their shirts on, assume that they would not, and return to my office with a clear conscience: I would have met the dean's request and could get on with my work. I thought the protest was rather clever because the ordinance did distinguish between women's and men's uncovered bodies and because the protesters were sitting quietly, reading and chatting. Certainly the fraternity members at the other end of the green didn't mind an audience of topless men and women.

It is important to note that although I was sympathetic to the topless protesters, I myself was fully clothed. Knowing I would be working well into the night on Friday and Saturday, I had dressed comfortably in a knit shirt, Laura Ashley jumper (remember, it *was* the late 1980s), and flat sandals. The jumper was a bright floral, kelly greens and blues with dashes of yellow, not unlike the daffodils waving in the sun on the green.

6

I left my office, walked onto the green, past congressional members and media, fraternity men on tricycles, parents and high school seniors, and over to the topless protesters. "I've been asked to come out and inform you that it is against municipal law for women to be shirtless in public," I said.

"We know that. And we think it's unfair. We'll put our shirts on when it gets cloudy or we get cold," replied an LGBA leader I knew well. "Did the dean send you out? And are they going to send Trikes for Tykes away, too?"

"Yes, he did, and no, I don't think anyone's talking to the Trikes guys. I'll let the dean know your stance on the shirts. Enjoy the sun, and stay safe this weekend. See you at the Big Gay Picnic on Sunday afternoon." And I turned to go. As I walked off the green, toward the sidewalk, I was feeling rather proud of myself. I had done my job—at least nominally—and had preserved my own sense of fairness. If frat boys can get drunk and ride tricycles, why can't women take off their shirts and sit in the sun? Is one a worse public image for recruiting new students and impressing congressional members? Feeling just a little cocky and self-righteous, I reached the edge of the grass, where a decorative chain border—maybe 15 inches high—prevented people from cutting the corner of the walkway and trampling the grass. The sun was out. Spring Weekend was off to a good start. I'd done my job with the topless students. I was feeling good about being in student affairs.

I hopped over the chain. Except that I didn't hop over the chain. I caught my sandal on the chain and fell, splayed out on the concrete, in a giant pool of Laura Ashley green and blue and yellow, like a flower delivery truck had tipped over and spilled its entire contents. For a moment, everything stopped. The congressional delegation froze in place as the university president whipped around to see what had happened. Parents and newly admitted students gasped. The tour guides covered their eyes, and the fraternity members stopped their trikes. At least that's how it felt. In reality, my knees were badly scraped and I bit my tongue when I landed. I lay on the ground for a few seconds, making sure nothing was broken.

Four topless women—all students I knew well, but not *that* well—bounded over to help me. "Oh, no, please! Really, I'm fine!" I proclaimed as they leaned over to help me up. "No, no. Really. *Don't!*" I pulled myself up to sitting, brushed off the gravel, and stood up, without help from the solicitous but shirtless students. I have often thought that even if I'd broken both legs, I would have found a way to get myself up off the sidewalk and into my office without their assistance.

The rest of Spring Weekend went fine. The clouds came out, the students put on their shirts and left, with invitations to many a fraternity party. The hearings ended and the camera crews left. Fourteen hundred new students enrolled the following fall, in spite (perhaps because) of the topless display during the campus tour. I bandaged my knees and tended to my wounded pride. The next year I wore a Spring Weekend t-shirt and jeans, with tennis shoes. I have never since, not once, attempted to hop over a pedestrian barrier, no matter how low. When graduate students and new professionals tell me they worry about how to do their jobs, how to balance their values with what they are sometimes asked to do as professionals, I think about myself, wiped out on the sidewalk, and chuckle just a little. "You'll figure it out," I say. "We all do eventually. Let me tell you about something in my past...."

I am an Educator

Stan Carpenter

I haven't given very many graduation speeches. When my students asked me to deliver a speech for our program graduates, parents, and friends, I was initially stumped. So that the parents and loved ones could finally know what their graduates were now destined to do, I decided to take on one of the hardest questions faced by student affairs professionals: What exactly do you do? Here is a short excerpt from that speech.

I want to let the parents and others in the room know the answer to the age-old question, "Now, what exactly do you mean by student affairs work?" Let me suggest that you begin to think of yourself by the broader term "educator."

You have earned a master's degree in education. Master means teacher, and this degree signifies your readiness to join in the education of undergraduates. A few of us teach in the traditional sense, in a classroom with a restricted subject matter. The rest facilitate. We cajole. We encourage. We model. We show. We lead. Our work is no less valuable for its apparent ephemeral nature. Each of you committed to this field because of your experience with others in your own education. You valued their efforts and wanted to influence students as you were influenced. In short, you are educators and heir to a long line of great minds and great spirits. It may seem in the 20th century that education as a profession is devalued, but a bit of reflection tells us otherwise. We educators are successors to Plato, who thought education the most important function of society; and Socrates, who refused to compromise in search of truth; and Aristotle, who showed that ideas are the true currency of immortality. All are teachers. All are educators. For the spiritually minded, Moses, Jesus, Buddha, Confucius, Mohammed—all were first and foremost teachers. There is an unbroken lineage from Augustinian to Thomas Aquinas to DaVinci to Newton to Luther to Horace Mann to Jane Hull to Esther Lloyd-Jones to Martin Luther King—and on and on—of great teachers who had great impact. In our heritage, we can trace our ideas from John Locke, who considered education to be the same as life; to Ben Franklin, who devoted his fortune to education; to Thomas Jefferson, who understood that only education would save the fledgling republic. You must understand your intellectual ancestors and learn to live up to the standards set by all the men and women who have gone before you as they created the finest system of higher education in the world. You have been touched by all those who went before, and you have been touched in your own educational lives by their heirs. Now we certify your readiness to join in the line. What an opportunity! What a responsibility! Education—

- Separates us from savagery

- Separates the pluralistic experiment known as the United States from other societies

- Empowers and allows democracy

- Allows humankind to survive, even though we have the capacity to destroy ourselves

- Pulls us from the dark chasms of racism and sexism and homophobia and all the other fearful, ignorant prejudices we harbor

To those who say that education is one of the problems in this country, I say, "You are wrong!" Education is the solution to our problems. The more we learn, the better off everyone will be.

John Dewey once said that philosophy is the general theory of education, so by extension, education would be applied philosophy. While this may be true, something I saw the other night makes me wonder. I was at my daughter's high school sports banquet. It was time to honor the spring athletes—the tennis team, the track team, the baseball team, and so on. The room was full of 15–18-year-olds. The hormones, muscles, and potential were palpable. For the first time, the banquet also included the Special Olympians. There were six. The first one laboriously made his way to the front and stood awkwardly as his accomplishments were extolled. He won a fourth in softball throw and a third in the 50-yard walk. He wore his medals around his neck and he cradled them in his hands as the crowd looked on. I cried—and I was not alone. After the six were honored and the earned awards were given to the other special athletes, the crowd rose for a standing ovation. I thought about education. The woman who worked with those kids was called coach, but not as we have been taught to think. Her job was not about winning, but about education. I thought about what those kids learned and what they taught a roomful of students and parents that night. Education may be applied philosophy, but it is also—and more importantly—applied love.

Something very much like this happens every day in student affairs. We encourage and lead our students to climb horrible and scary mountains, and then we help them down. Sometimes they slip and fall, and sometimes they even die. Sometimes they just wish they would. Sure, they fail—but we help them get ready for the next try. We have an impact on society, one student at a time, and who knows what good may come if we can do it well and if we never forget, not for a minute, that what we do matters greatly.

So, the next time someone you meet asks you what you do, don't hem and haw as we all do in student affairs, knowing they won't easily understand. Instead, draw yourself up, look them in the eye, and say:

"I am a guardian of democracy;
I carry the water of life for our society;
I am the bearer of compassion and concern, the dispeller
of pessimism and hatred;
I am the bringer of fire to the mind and hope to the heart;
I am the herald of love to all who will listen, to all who would learn.
I am an Educator!"

Don't Take Yourself Too Seriously

Doris Ching

Shortly after I became a vice president for student affairs, I was invited to introduce the keynote speaker at a statewide convention of women educators. Wow! What a great honor, to address an august group of the most dignified and respected women educators in the state. It was not only a privilege, it was a big deal. I wanted to do a good job. After all, the keynote speaker, Dr. Henry Mitchell, was a highly intelligent professor and competent researcher, well-known as the state's most astute analyst on local and national politics and elections. More important, I was extremely grateful to Dr. Mitchell, who had helped the convention in our lobbying efforts to influence important state legislation that would benefit students. Like everyone else, I had known of his political savvy, and, through our lobbying collaboration, I grew to respect him even more deeply for the time and insights he generously shared. I was touched by his genuine kindness and sincere desire to help the group succeed with legislation that would secure greater financial aid for graduate and undergraduate students.

Dr. Mitchell rarely smiled. He always looked pensive and serious. His walk was slow and deliberate, his diminutive stature hunched over, his eyes staring straight ahead through thick, black-rimmed glasses. He was reticent. Although he was widely respected for his brilliant mind and extraordinary knowledge, very few knew that he was also a kind-hearted, warm, inspiring, and charming person. Introducing him at the convention was auspicious. I welcomed the opportunity to acknowledge publicly his invaluable assistance to the organization. I was determined to reveal the warm and gracious side of Dr. Mitchell in the introduction. After giving the matter much serious thought, a fantastic idea popped into my head. I would compare Dr. Mitchell to my favorite vegetable. I got up before the crack of dawn the morning of the convention and, in anticipation of the important event, I carefully wrote my introductory remarks.

The audience was an awesome group. At the podium, I faced the state's most dedicated women educators, most of them gray-haired and some nearly twice my age. Many had retired from their professional positions and continued to be influential in statewide educational policy. My former sixth grade teacher sat in the front row. My 10th grade English teacher smiled at me from the third row. I was humbled by the esteemed group of intelligent, dignified, and very proper women leaders. I felt dwarfed by their immense collective knowledge and experiences. Fortunately, I was well-prepared for my task. I calmly proceeded to introduce the distinguished speaker. I confidently began, "Dr. Mitchell reminds me of my favorite vegetable—the artichoke. Like the artichoke, with Dr. Mitchell, I start at the top (his brain), where I find wonderful and delightful nourishment, and the lower I go, the more delightful it gets…" I then heard a roar so loud, I thought the roof of the auditorium had fallen. The thunder of laughter prevented me from finishing the sentence. My mouth dropped. I was stunned. As the last of the guffaws and chuckles finally subsided, I barely recovered from the unplanned mirth, and with a face as red as a beet, I finished the sentence, "…until I reach the heart." By then, my brilliant analogy was a wash, and my good intentions were totally ruined. The women would not stop laughing, and they seemed not to care that *the top* was his brilliant mind and *the lower* was his kind heart! A week later, the president of the organization sent me a beautiful children's book on *How to Eat An Artichoke*.

From time to time throughout my student affairs career, unintentionally, I made a fool of myself. It was fortuitous that I was once an eighth grade English teacher and realized, to my delight, that I had the mentality and level of humor of an eighth grader. I discovered that the combination was an asset to a student affairs administrator in higher education. It created an ideal state of mind, soul, and spirit. It saved me from falling apart in unexpected incidents such as the artichoke introduction. Moreover, it kept me motivated, stimulated, and optimistic as a vice president for student affairs. The lessons I gained as an eighth grade teacher and a senior student affairs officer were invaluable.

13

Lesson No. 1: Laugh at anything and everything—especially yourself—and, absolutely, don't linger on things that go wrong. I recovered relatively quickly from the embarrassment of the artichoke incident because I could laugh at myself and not dwell on the faux pas. The willingness to laugh at myself has been my saving grace in numerous situations. Students of all ages appreciate humanness in an administrator. They were more forgiving of my small, stupid blunders when I readily admitted my shortcomings and laughed at myself, rather than attempting to cover up my mistakes with inane excuses.

Lesson No. 2: Be realistic. No one remembers the profound things; they only remember the dumb things. I should have known better than to inform my eighth graders that I had mistakenly picked up the wrong canister that morning and sprayed Hadabug insect repellant on my hair, thinking it was hair spray. Every morning thereafter, for the rest of the year, the students inspected my hair for flies and gnats. Years later, those students' fondest memory of their eighth grade English class was the Hadabug incident, rather than my superb teaching. How naïve I was to think I might be remembered for my masterful teaching. How unreasonable of me to *expect* students to be aware of my efforts to help them learn. I would have been prudent to appreciate even the smallest acknowledgment. Interestingly, the unanticipated result of my philosophical shift is that I now receive letters and messages each year from students who write in gratitude of contributions I made to their educational success decades ago. It surprises me that they remember, long after I myself had forgotten what I did that would deserve their thanks.

Lesson No. 3: Forget trying to direct students and allow them to take the lead. My favorite hat has two visors, one facing right and the other facing left. Inscribed on the hat is the question I asked myself constantly, "I'm their leader; which way did they go?" Indeed, on many occasions, as I contemplated possible solutions to address a campus issue, the student government officers had already decided on the best solution, taken action, moved in the right direction, and were on their way to resolving the matter. It is no wonder that many of them are now statespersons in public office and leaders in business and industry.

Lesson No. 4: Don't take yourself too seriously because no one else does. I am blessed to have had the most stimulating and best job ever. Working daily with students provided endless rewarding moments and spiritual self-renewal opportunities. For added personal renewal, I included physical exercise in my routine, with a jog-and-conference with a colleague at 5:30 a.m. around the university track. Three times a week, I would get into a pair of old shorts, tank top, and oversized windbreaker; throw a change of clothes onto the back seat of the car; and, with hair barely combed, drive off to meet my colleague. One morning, I felt especially pleased with myself and smiled as I drove down the highway, visualizing the day ahead. After the jog, I would shower, get into my clothes, and transform into the university vice president I was expected to look like. I looked forward to visiting the residence halls, admiring the clean and bright halls all ready for the arrival of the new freshmen. I would then put the finishing touches on my welcome remarks at the New Student Orientation. Great events. Yes, it will be a great day. When I looked in the rear view mirror, I saw a blue light flashing and revolving on the car behind me. I pulled over, took out my driver's license and presented it to the big, burly officer in uniform. Aware that I tend to drive faster when I am excited, I apologized profusely, "I'm very sorry, officer. I was thinking about the day and unaware I was speeding." I was hoping the officer would see the name on my driver's license and recognize it. After all, I was an executive of our state university. Instead, the officer looked at me, then at my strewn clothes on the backseat, and asked, "Are you employed?"

Somehow, I convinced him that I, indeed, had a job and a home. But, before he walked back to his car, he warned, "Next time, think more about your driving and speeding than the events of the day." I was embarrassed, but relieved that I was not issued a citation. That incident was my wake-up call that there is no place for self-importance—anytime and anywhere.

Lesson No. 5: Forget about your own ego. You can't have one. I threw my ego out the window years ago. Without the ego, I became a better educator and student affairs administrator. Without the ego, I remained ever humble. Without the ego, I could laugh at myself. I would be forgiven by students for my inept mistakes. I *appreciated* rather than *expected* acknowledgment by students of any good deed I might have done. I empowered students to lead. I was constantly reminded not to take myself too seriously. Without the ego, I enjoyed funny and rewarding times as a student affairs administrator.

The Power of Four:
The Delta-P Sisterhood

Michelle Asha Cooper, Kathleen Lis Dean,
Michele C. Murray, and Heather Rowan-Kenyon

The shelves of university and chain bookstores are full of titles such as *Surviving Your Dissertation, How to Complete and Survive a Doctoral Dissertation*, and *The Portable Dissertation Advisor*. These books and others like them respond to an anxiety common to many doctoral students. The dissertation—if one makes it that far—is a lonely, challenging process that proves nearly impossible to complete and leaves many bright graduate students with the suffix ABD.

Each of us, in her own way, had these fears. Contemplating just one dissertation was, well…intimidating. Had anyone suggested that to make it through the finish line, we would have to live through not one but *four* dissertations, none of us would have enrolled in that first class. Ironically, though, without the other three experiences, none of us would have completed her own dissertation.

We found strength and confidence in a four-way friendship that occurred by chance, or perhaps by providence. Our names are Heather, Kathleen, Michele, and Michelle. We call ourselves Delta-P. This is our story. We hope it inspires others to cherish their communities of support, the people without whom success would not be possible.

IN THE BEGINNING...

We met in 2001 on the first day of the first class in our doctoral program. Two of us were full-time students with assistantships in the division of student affairs, and two of us worked full time in the field. Nothing about our previous or current experiences indicated that we would become the keys to survival for one another.

The first encounter started like any other first-day-of-school experience: with smiles, friendly greetings, and course syllabi. Nothing appeared out of the ordinary or particularly remarkable, save the intimidation and doubt that silently plagued each of us.

Heather, Michele, and Michelle remember as if it were yesterday:

> Kathleen introduced herself and said that she was interested in studying leadership teams. She was so intrigued by the topic that she woke up at 4:00 a.m. that particular morning to finish reading a new text on the subject. For the three of us, that was the moment our hearts sank! Kathleen embodied our idea of the quintessential doctoral student, and since no academic reading was likely to awaken us from deep sleep, we were suddenly convinced that we did not have the right stuff.

For her part, Kathleen was just as nervous. She recalls:

> As the transfer student with a year of classes under my belt, I found myself among many first-year doctoral students. While I had already overcome most of my fears about doing doctoral work, I was nervous about starting at a new school, with new faculty, and finding the friends and support I knew I would need. I felt like an outsider.

In the beginning, we were strangers to one another—people who happened to enroll in the same program at the same time. Other than sharing a class and an academic interest in higher education, we were so different from one another. In retrospect, perhaps it was our differences, and not our commonalities, that drew us together. As the proverb says, "Necessity is the mother of all invention," and so it was with us. Each of us needed peer support to get the most out of our program, and out of this need we "invented" a highly functional peer network.

A SISTERHOOD IS BORN

Ours was not a cohort system—we did not travel in a pack. However, at least two of us, and often three or four of us, were in class together.

Over multiple semesters we found ourselves slowly developing a system of support that would prove to be invaluable once the classes were over and the solitude of the dissertation began. Semester after semester, we found we needed one another to be better students. We processed ideas and experiences, we encouraged one another to think big thoughts, and we challenged one another to stretch intellectually and professionally. Whenever possible, we seized the opportunity to work together. We always knew that we could count on each other to do good work and carry out our respective responsibilities. We also carried the load for each other when needed, knowing that someone would carry the load for us at some point on this journey.

One notable moment occurred for Heather and Kathleen in an education policy analysis course. This gateway course for the doctoral program was a challenge for everyone. If you made it through successfully, the odds of completing the dissertation were favorable. Heather and Kathleen took this course together, during their second semester, and found it overwhelming and a real jolt of reality.

> We were finally experiencing a doctoral-level class. This was a real test of our ability to survive the doctorate, and we were worried that we wouldn't be able to get through it. The writing was intense, and the rewriting expectations were high. The only way we got through the academic and mental challenge was together—by proofreading, suggesting ideas, providing moral support and sometimes a shoulder to cry on.

Our intervention in one another's school lives ranged from the mundane to the miraculous. In addition to providing feedback for each other's work, we made sure each of us was on track for success. As the part-time student whose full-time life was an hour away, Michele relied on her full-time classmates to keep her up to speed with the department news and to remind her when to register for classes.

All of us had very full and involved lives, and school was just another dimension. If we weren't careful, our worlds would collide. Without realizing it, we were developing coping mechanisms that required active participation from the group. Michelle found herself in this predicament a few times and finally yelled for help.

Because I was generous to a fault with my time, I asked the group for help, and they instituted a permission-slip policy. Every time I wanted to volunteer or do something beyond work and school, I had to ask for "permission." Essentially, one of these women would help me weigh the options and would advise about whether the new commitment was a good use of my time. Although it might seem awkward and childish, it was a tremendous help.

By our third semester together, we were subscribing to the motto "economy of effort" and beginning to focus our course work and extracurricular activities on projects that could lead to dissertation-length research. We were in the habit of working together in small groups and learning how to play off of each other's strengths. We often met at Heather's place near campus or for dinner to go over syllabi or dive more deeply into class discussion topics. The process of forming as a group was organic, almost unintentional, and it made the doctoral process fun.

The true test of the sisterhood came in the last class the four of us shared: policy and applied statistics. This was a class unlike any other in our program. We learned advanced statistics while sorting through policy issues in education. Heather, Kathleen, and Michelle worked in one group, while Michele partnered with another classmate. Still, the four of us spent countless hours on the phone trying to resolve our own questions before breaking down and calling the teaching assistant for help. It was in one of these four-way conference calls that we became the "Delta-Ps."

In statistics, *delta-p* is the change in probability for an outcome. It's a pretty simple concept, really, but try as we might, none of us could figure it out. After several days of phone and in-person consultation, we were mortified to learn that unlike most of the other statistical concepts we were using, *delta-p* required no particular mental gymnastics to understand. From then on, *delta-p* became a metaphor for our little foursome: It didn't take much to understand how well it worked. In fact, we could say that the relationship we had formed had changed the probability of our success for the better.

ONE PART, THREE PARTS, FOUR PARTS DONE: THE DISSERTATIONS AND BEYOND

The commitment to one another's success made all the difference. People ask us how we managed to downplay the sense of competition that often creeps into these types of relationships. We always shrug and say that all along we encouraged each other by committing to the idea that we would not be done with our degree program until the very last one of us crossed the stage at graduation.

Michele developed a simple arithmetic for marking our progression through the program: We were 33% complete when all of us passed our comprehensive exam, and then 66% complete when we passed our dissertation proposals. Finally, we would be 100% complete once all of us graduated. We were sure to celebrate each milestone as if it were the last.

As the trailblazer, Heather set the stage for everyone who followed:

> I was the first to successfully defend a dissertation proposal and final dissertation. At times, I felt bad having everyone read multiple drafts of my work while I was not doing that for the others. I was reminded that soon enough it would be my turn to read their drafts. I know that my finished product was much stronger due to the insight of these three women.

Despite being "finished," Heather did not feel as though her work was done. We reexamined our math and developed a more complicated equation to account for the reality of four individuals' staggered progress. One hundred percent completion was still the goal, but we began to divide our three-phase process equally among the four of us. Heather's graduation, then, added to all of us having passed our comps, and three more of us passing our dissertation proposals meant that as a group we had achieved 66% full completion and we were working steadily to meet our goal. Given the crazy math here, it's no wonder we call ourselves Delta-P! We vowed that we were not done until we were all done. So, we slowly but surely calculated our progress to 100%.

We redoubled our efforts. We applied the same care with which we handled Heather's dissertation and defense preparation to the three that followed. Over the next 2 years, we read and commented on drafts. We provided a sounding board for findings and potential findings. We conducted mock defenses. We anticipated questions the committees might pose, and then we worked together until the person in the "hot seat" found the appropriate answers. The insights we provided one another helped us cover more research ground; in many cases, we were tougher on each other than our committees were. Certainly, our team approach helped each of us understand her research more deeply than if she had prepared alone.

In the midst of the dissertation frenzy, we all had experiences that made us realize that life and living don't take a backseat to graduate school. On the heels of a miscarriage, Kathleen learned that her advisor and first-choice dissertation chair was joining the faculty at another institution.

> I couldn't believe that this was happening to me! The faculty member I had transferred to the University of Maryland to work with was moving. In addition to losing one of my best teachers, I was faced with the rapidly approaching dissertation without an advisor. I learned this news right before one of my classes, and the shock of it all sent me running out of the classroom in tears. If it weren't for the support of Heather, Michelle, and Michele, I would have wallowed in my misery. Instead, we regrouped and I went forward with the search for a new advisor, relying on this foursome for the feedback and guidance I needed in the meantime.

It was the sisterhood that helped Kathleen regain her spirits and the confidence to continue. It was the sisterhood that supported Michelle when a member of her family was killed in a drunk-driving accident.

> During my final year of the program—while writing my dissertation—I faced several personal tragedies. The first was that my sister-in-law was tragically killed by a drunk driver. This was a shocking and overwhelmingly sad time for me and my family. However, the sadness didn't stop there. Over the next year, my aunt, uncle, and family dog also suddenly died. It was a very difficult time, one where I was often sad, distracted, and/or angry. In spite of it all, the dissertation was written. While I attribute this success to many factors, one was the sisterhood. They were a source of

support for me and my family, offering encouragement every step along the way.

It was the sisterhood that conspired to host a cocktail party at Kathleen's house and throw Heather into a matchmaking social situation. Heather married that man 2 years later, and we toasted the sisterhood. Over the years, we have seen each other through births, marriages, cross-country moves, multiple job changes, and accolades. We were there for each others' defenses, and we celebrated each one together, alongside our families and our faculty.

As we finished our dissertations, and in one case beforehand, some of us moved away. Michele moved to Seattle, and Kathleen headed to Ohio.

We were all determined that this geographic interruption would not deter us. I [Kathleen] was so proud to fly back to the East Coast within that next year to attend the defenses of Michele and Michelle. Later, I was so grateful when they returned the favor and traveled for mine, the last one.

We are now sprinkled across the country, following different professional pursuits: two as assistant vice presidents for student affairs, one as a faculty member in a student affairs preparation program, and one as the president of a higher education policy institute. Despite the distance, we still enjoy the bond. We helped each other become better scholars and professionals. We pushed one another to achieve and accomplish goals we may have been too timid to explore. Above all, we have become friends.

Even though we do not live close to one another as we once did, we are still a strong support network. We have read cover letters, done mock interviews, and provided a listening ear for work challenges. Sometimes we are lucky enough to have our professional lives bring us together on projects or committees, but the sisterhood relies on the personal connection we share.

What is the secret to our success? We checked our egos at the door. We realized early on that each of us has talent and that we had more to gain by working together than engaging in debilitating competition. It is a choice we made to help rather than hinder and to take the time to be more than classmates—to build friendships that lasted beyond the classroom.

As a faculty member now, Heather sees a lot of students come and go through the graduate program. She reflects:

> In the student affairs profession, we promote collaboration and teamwork to help undergraduate students learn, develop, and grow in college. While we promote that in others, at times it is forgotten when we think about developing ourselves. As graduate students, we realized that we were all good, strong students and professionals, and that we had more to gain by working together than by putting each other down in order to be at the top.

Looking back, we feel so lucky to have formed this special bond with one another. We share our story so that others may be inspired to act similarly. Here's to peer support! Here's to the sisterhood! All hail, Delta-P!

FRATERNITY HOUSE BREAK-IN

JAMES D. HARDWICK

"There has been a break-in in one of your fraternity houses," the police officer told me over the phone.

It was my first day of work as the new associate director of campus programs and organizations, and the college's fraternity and sorority advisor. I grabbed a legal pad and a pen so I could take notes. I knew that this position, on a campus with a strong fraternity and sorority presence, would be challenging, but I did not expect to receive a phone call from the police on my first day of work. Knowing that the college-owned fraternity houses were unoccupied during the summer months, I braced myself for the bad news.

"Apparently, some local kids broke into the fraternity house through a basement window. We entered the house to see if there was any damage or vandalism," the officer explained. "The kids apparently broke into the chapter room of the fraternity house. I need you to know that we found some unusual items."

Thinking through all the possible "unusual items" that could be found in a fraternity basement—let alone a fraternity's chapter room—I asked the officer what he found. The response I received caught me off guard.

"We think we found satanic worship equipment," the officer said quietly. "You know—equipment that you would use to worship the devil."

I paused and let this information sink in. "Satanic worship equipment in the fraternity's chapter room?" I began to have a suspicion that the local kids may have discovered the fraternity's ritual equipment.

I asked the officer what exactly he found. The officer prefaced reading the list of items on his incident report with an apology that his ac-

24

cusation of satanic worship equipment in the fraternity basement may have been made too hastily. He offered to read the list of items to me and so I could tell him if these items would typically be found in a fraternity house.

"The first thing we found were robes—hooded robes," the officer said. I immediately realized the images of devil worship that must have gone through the mind of the police officer before he placed the phone call to the college. I told the police officer that hooded robes can be found in a fraternity house. I explained that the fraternity members may wear robes during their ceremonies and meetings. I told him that the robes may be similar to the robes that would be found in a church choir.

"We also found a wooden altar. The altar had lots of melted candle wax on the top," the officer reported. "The strange thing was that there was a Bible on the altar. Devil worshippers typically would not have a Christian Bible on the altar if they were involved in satanic worship."

I agreed with the officer that a Christian Bible would be out of place with devil worshippers. I assured him that a fraternity could use an altar in their rituals. I suggested that the Bible might have been left open to an important verse for the fraternity or, if found closed, used to administer oaths.

"We also found all of these booklets with speaking parts in them."

I asked the officer if any of the booklets talked about the devil. He replied that he looked through the booklets and found references to values, brotherhood, fraternity, and oaths. He said that he even found references to Jesus Christ and Bible verses in the booklets. He reported that he did not see any references to Satan or the devil. I explained to the officer that these booklets were likely used by the fraternity to conduct ceremonies and meetings.

"We also found one more disturbing thing, but I expect that you will have a reasonable explanation for the item," the officer reported. "We found a human skull. But I bet you are going to tell me that having a skull in these meetings may be within the range of possibilities."

I told the officer that a skull could sometimes be found in fraternity insignia. The skull might represent fraternity brothers who died or remind the members that the oaths they took lasted until death. I could hear the sigh of relief on the other end of the phone after he heard my explanation. I am not sure if the officer heard my own sigh of relief.

The police officer thanked me for my help. He offered to call our college facilities department to have them board the basement window until the window could be replaced. He said that he would notify his department's patrol officers to watch the fraternity complex for other break-ins over the remainder of the summer until the students were back as residents.

I thanked the police officer for his phone call. I told him that I appreciated the fact that he called about the items he had found in the fraternity house. I said that if he had any further incidents involving our fraternities or sororities, I would appreciate a phone call. I replaced the receiver on the phone and caught my breath. I had survived my first incident as a fraternity and sorority advisor.

From Tragedy to Hope: Illuminating the Darkness

Les P. Cook and Christopher L. Haddix

Much like the famous sports show *ABC's Wide World of Sports*, the stories that occur on our campuses often illustrate the thrill of victory as well as the agony of defeat. We are taught to celebrate accomplishment, learn from mistakes, and work through difficulty. Our work in student affairs provides us numerous opportunities to celebrate success. However, occasionally we are required to attend to darker situations, when there seems to be no trace of light, such as a student's tragic death at the hand of another student.

This dual first-person narrative is written from the point of view of the student convicted of causing another's death in a drunk driving accident and the administrator who handled the incident. For the families of those injured and deceased, the shadows may endure forever. However, our commitment to educate and develop students and to find a glimmer of hope was not alleviated by a legal conviction—but rather intensified by it.

DR. COOK:

My wife woke me at 3:45 a.m. The call was from public safety. There was a hit and run where one student was severely injured and another killed. My gut wrenched. Soon after the call, a suspect, another one of our students, was located.

When I received the call, I had been the vice provost and dean for only 2 months. Unfortunately, I came to realize that no matter how long we are on the job, no one is ever truly prepared to deal with tragedies involving our students.

Luckily, these types of misfortunes do not happen frequently on our campus, and while inevitably heartbreaking, it is important to recognize the fact that we can learn from tragedy. The driver of the vehicle, Chris, was arraigned soon after the accident and allowed to continue with his schooling for the fall and spring semesters. He was subsequently sentenced to 2–5 years in a state prison for leaving the scene of an accident that resulted in serious impairment and death.

Upon his sentencing, Chris's father asked if we would ever allow him to return and complete his degree. I told him that we viewed college as an educational process, and as long as Chris learned from this tragedy, we would consider his reinstatement upon his release from prison. In doing this, I believe that our community gave Chris hope and, in some ways, the strength to get through the ordeal of prison and to get his life back on track.

Over the course of the next 3 years, I maintained periodic correspondence with Chris and his parents. The letters between us were honest, emotional, and hopeful. I shared with him information about how things were going on campus and my optimism for his return. He shared his remorse, sincerity, and hopes for the future. As I watched our on-campus students enjoy each day, my heart ached for Chris as I imagined how different his daily routine must have been.

Chris was released from prison in May 2007. Soon thereafter, we talked on the phone and made plans to reenroll him. During the summer, Chris made a trip to campus and we connected for the first time in person. I felt as though I had known him for most of my life and was relieved that the walls that he knew for the past 3 years were now behind him.

After returning to campus, Chris did exceedingly well, both in college and in life. He made the dean's list each semester, was actively involved in research, and graduated. In Chris I see a young man who is incredibly bright and passionate, and is willing to do what he can to make a difference in our world. He learned from his past, is committed to being a positive contributor to society, and is enthused about the future.

CHRIS:

It has been more than 5 years now since the night in late September 2003 when I ended a young man's life prematurely and seriously injured a second individual as well by driving drunk. The absolutely crushing realization that hit me, while handcuffed in the back of a police car, was that the poor decisions I made in my life—my own actions—were responsible for another man's death. I ended a life. I caused an unfathomable amount of pain to the family of the victims, my own family, and the lives of all those involved in the incident. It was a long time before I could look into a mirror and see anything in the reflection that provided me with a reason to live.

After the accident, I carried on for quite some time in a state of almost ethereal perpetuity, attending classes without a true desire to be there. I expected the pervasive sense of guilt and shame to diminish, but as I would learn in the coming years, some things only slightly dissipate with time. I managed to complete the rest of the fall semester in good standing and even held on through the spring semester without completely abandoning the notion that furthering my education was somehow inherently important.

Upon entrance into the State of Michigan's Department of Corrections, I had only a vague idea of what the following years would entail. I was ashamed and completely reticent. With a future in doubt, ruined lives in my past, and an unspecified amount of time to be spent in prison, the possibility that something positive might be likely in the years to come was an idea that I was loath to entertain. I deserved to be in prison, and the consequences of my actions were the only appropriate way that I could accept responsibility for my behavior. My actions had a devastating effect upon the lives of others, and no specific action would ever be able to rectify my previous transgressions.

Although I began my time in prison with the knowledge that I would never be able to fully repay my debt to the family of the deceased, I gradually became aware of the positive influence that I could have upon the lives of others. It was incredibly hard for me at first to find an authentic reason to persevere as a productive member of society, but that began to change after I received news from my father that Michigan Tech would possibly reinstate me as a student at the university. I entered into a tutoring job at the prison and began to help other prisoners study to attain a general equivalency diploma. I cannot begin to describe the sense of satisfaction and worth that came from helping others in their quests to become more educated. Even though it was not possible for me to directly repay the debt I owed to my victim's family, it was becoming evident that I could at least impart some degree of positive change upon the world.

I continued to be a tutor for most of my time in prison and developed friendships with a variety of individuals who sought to somehow improve their lives. I gradually began to improve my life as well. I exercised frequently and developed friendships with people who had accepted responsibility for their crimes and devoted themselves to becoming better individuals. I improved my own knowledge of what it meant to lead a productive life.

The catalyst for the change that occurred within me was the knowledge that some people in the "outside" community had not given up on me. The support of Dr. Cook and the rest of the academic community were instrumental in providing me with a reason to carry on, pick up the pieces, and aim toward a future in which I could be proud. I always wanted to finish my degree, and with a little hard work and perseverance, I found that as long as I did not give up on myself, the rest of the world might just support me in that effort. The communications I had with Dr. Cook while I was in prison were enlightening. I encountered an individual, whom I barely knew, who exhibited optimism at my chances of reintegrating into society and making something of myself. I have him—and the many others who did not lose faith in me—to thank for the fact that I did not slip completely into a downward spiral of depression and give up on achieving a college education.

DR. COOK:

While it may be an extreme example, Chris's story is the curriculum of student affairs. Its classrooms, lessons, and laboratories are often beyond our control, but it's our job to maneuver the elements we've been given to build the best possible outcome for our students. Sometimes, students like Chris hand us the syllabus for the most important lessons they will ever learn, and we must be prepared to teach that lesson.

As our days fill with minutiae, we must not forget how vitally important it is to connect with and support our students. We need to ask ourselves daily, "If not me, who?" We must be unwilling to concede a missed learning opportunity and always search for the hope within the tragedy. Chris taught me that where there seems to be no light at all, there is light to be had. I have become a pupil of his, just as he is a pupil of mine.

First Generation:
Understanding the Symbols

Cheryl Daly

I was teaching a course, Problems in Urban Education, to senior undergraduate students at a large, urban public university. Most of the students in my class were African Americans or students of African descent. This particular day, a student approached me excited about preparing for an interview for the teacher education graduate program at the university. He asked if I would help him prepare. We practiced questions about his teaching philosophy, why he wanted to be a teacher, what he would contribute to the lives of his students, and so on. The student eventually felt prepared for the interview.

A week later, the student came to my office and announced that he had just completed his interview a few hours before and thought he did a super job. I noticed that the student was wearing a very stylish cardigan sweater rather than a shirt and tie. I asked, "Why did you wear a sweater and not a shirt and tie to the interview?"

He responded, "What do you mean? Bill Cosby doesn't wear a shirt and tie, and he's a doctor! Can you think of a better role model to imitate? I was trying to look like an educated professional." I laughed out loud. I looked very empathically at the student with a warm smile. I replied, "Bill Cosby is a fine role model, but Bill Cosby, EdD, as Dr. Cliff Huxtable, was acting in the comforts of his TV home. You, on the other hand, just interviewed in front of the teacher education program recruitment committee." The student assured me that the next time he interviewed for a position he would wear a shirt and tie.

Three weeks later, I had my own "role-modeling moment." I had to follow the lead of someone I admired and was convinced that the person played by the rules. I knew if I followed her lead, success would be imminent.

While attending my doctoral graduation ceremony, I noticed an honorary degree recipient, a prominent African American woman, was holding her cap in her hand. She did not wear the cap when she received her award. I also noticed that two other Black women faculty members on stage were not wearing their caps. I proceeded to take off my cap and proudly hold it in my hand. I thought, surely these women must be displaying some form of "sisterhood of academic wisdom." I even took my graduation picture with my cap in my hand.

Later I found out why all three women, whom I admired, had not worn their caps. It was simple: Their caps would not fit over their corn rolls. Their hats were too small, and not wearing them had nothing to do with sisterhood or wisdom. In my learning moment, I laughed out loud. As a first-generation graduate student trying to find my way in an age-old system, I misread one of the symbols. Learning can be laugh-out-loud funny.

Lifted Up in France

Lee Burdette Williams

Every medieval city in France has a cathedral. Le Puy-en-Velay had one, a mammoth Romanesque structure with an apparently infinite number of steps. As I stood at their foot, I realized I would not, in my weary state, be able to climb them. Without warning, though, I felt strong hands lifting me from below my elbows and literally carrying me up the stairs.

On either side of me was a student—Tommy on one side, Alan on the other. Chapin and Cannon right behind. Four students lifted me and carried me through one of the worst weeks of my career.

One would think that spring break spent in France would be a delightful and interesting experience. I completed a similar trip to Italy the previous year with the same professor. She was a friend who invited me along, in part because I was "good with students." She was the brains of the outfit, the religion scholar who designed a class around the prominent religious sites and traditions of the country. The trip to Italy was great, so I readily signed on for another 10 days, another 25 students, another country.

The trip had an inauspicious start, as recruitment didn't go as well as planned. By the time we departed, we had just 18 students in our care. Six of them, including the four stair-carriers, were members of the residential college I directed. I felt pretty good about the group, knowing a third of them quite well. I also knew and trusted my colleague, who spent the better part of the winter scouring the Internet and planning an ideal itinerary full of great sites and powerful learning.

A couple weeks before our departure date, my husband's mother, who had been ill for quite a while, took a turn for the worse. She passed away the weekend before our departure. I told my father-in-law that I was going to back out of the trip, but he convinced me that his wife (like him, a lifelong educator) would want no such thing. "You have a commitment to your students, and she would not want you to back out." So with his encouragement and my husband's support, I boarded a plane the day before her funeral.

We flew into Paris and took a high-speed train south to Arles. During our first night, my colleague and roommate mentioned she was not feeling well. She had had some health issues when we traveled to Italy, so I wasn't too concerned. Her general complaints continued the next day and evening. She was experiencing a rapid heart rate, digestive issues, and a generally miserable disposition.

In addition to my colleague's questionable health early on, we had a major behavioral situation with two students in a small village inn that resulted in a justifiably harsh complaint from the inn owner to Simon, our trip guide. My colleague and I decided to confront the students once we had them together on the bus. I am not, by nature, much of a yeller. My colleague, though, wasn't feeling up to the challenge, and so it fell to me to let them have it. I told them that any one of them could be sent home if they couldn't manage to behave in the ways we had repeatedly requested. My six students looked at me wide-eyed (none of them were involved in the incident), knowing me well enough to see through the act. They played along, bless their hearts, as we headed from Carcassonne to Roquefort. The bus was quiet, except for an occasional moan from one of the students involved in the previous evening's alcohol-stoked festivities.

About an hour into the ride, feeling a little guilty, I got up from my seat at the front of the bus and went back to sit with the students I knew. They seemed happy to see me, and we had a fun conversation about the discovery of bleu cheese and other serendipitous acts that have changed civilization. They told me, too, that they had come up with a nickname for me. "Ace!" Alan said brightly. They all smiled, but avoided eye contact with me. I knew the nickname was about something other than my long-ago softball pitching prowess. I didn't press the issue. I was just happy to be enjoying their company, even happier that they seemed to be enjoying mine.

We arrived at Le Puy-en-Velay a few hours later, and things quickly fell apart. My colleague decided that her health was enough of a concern that she needed to seek a doctor's care. Simon had the hotel clerk call for an ambulance, and off they went to a hospital. I knew then how this would turn out: My colleague was going to leave me in France with 18 students expecting three credits of academic content. Despite my rising panic, I accompanied the students down the street to the steps of Cathedral Notre Dame. I looked up at the daunting staircase, near tears, wondering how I could make my *own* exit from this debacle. That's when I was suddenly lifted and carried to the top of the steps. "We got ya, Ace," Alan said, as they deposited me outside the door. We walked together into the cathedral, where I found a quiet spot and managed to pull myself into a reasonable state of mind and heart.

My colleague returned from the hospital that night and announced her plans to depart from the airport in Lyon in the morning. She spent most of the night on the phone with her mother, her travel agent, and the travel insurance agent, planning her escape. I tried to sleep, but between her agitated conversations and my own frustration and fear, it was impossible. The next morning we detoured to Lyon, and Simon and I saw her off while the students waited on the bus. We walked out of the terminal and climbed the steps of the bus. I looked up the aisle at 18 anxious faces. "Okay, then, folks. We're down one instructor, but you still have me and Simon." The students looked back at me. A few of them smiled. Others nodded and returned to their music. Alan, Chapin, Tommy, and Cannon cheered. "Yeah, Ace! Ace is in charge!" They knew me well enough to tease me, and even better, they knew I needed some fun.

I'm not sure what the four of them discussed among themselves, but the truth was, I wasn't in charge as much as one would have thought. They were, and they were very good at it.

That afternoon, we headed for a lovely town called Vezelay. As we rode along beautiful roads in this very rural part of France, I furiously studied my two guidebooks. I was at the front of the group. As we approached the entrance to this beautiful church, I stopped and looked up at the sculptures on the arches above the door. I began parroting back what the guidebooks had said about these works of art, about the relics of Mary Magdalene inside, a bit lost in my own reverie. When I turned around, the students were gathered around me, listening more intently than they had to any of our much-more-knowledgeable local guides, even to my colleague, whose knowledge far surpassed mine. I finished my very brief lesson, and the group applauded, led by the Sweet Boys (as I had started calling them in my journal). "Yeah, Ace!" they said. "Way to go with the info!"

That night we pulled into the town of Nimes, where we were scheduled to stay at a small, family-owned hotel. The group wasn't even in the door when the owner, a woman who apparently was a prison matron in a former life, began dressing down my students as though they had already trashed her lovely place. Bewildered, I looked at Simon, who then spoke to her in French and listened while she yelled at him. He then reported to me, "She said they didn't know this was a group of college students when it was booked, and that they never book groups of college students because they behave so badly." I sighed and shook my head, then looked as imploringly at the students as I could.

"We've got it covered, Ace," said Cannon. I'm not entirely sure what threats they used with the others, particularly the two who had been difficult throughout the trip, but it must have worked. I wished that their magic extended to my immune system. By midnight, I found myself exhibiting symptoms of a quickly arriving head cold, unable to lie down without my sinuses filling like a sink. It was another sleepless night. By morning, I was miserably sick. We climbed aboard the bus for Chartres, and Simon, who by then was about to write off all American women as weak and troublesome creatures, promised to help me find medicine once we arrived. While the students toured yet another cathedral, Simon and I visited a local pharmacy where I tried to explain my need for cold medicine that didn't contain pseudoephedrine, which makes me jittery and sleepless. That particular word—"pseudoephedrine"—is not in most phrase books. Nonetheless, I managed to get what I needed—the world's most powerful cold medicine, apparently. Within 20 minutes of taking it, I was practically comatose, and stayed that way for the ride to Paris.

I guess for a lot of people Paris is a dream destination. For me it simply meant a bed and, more important, two free days during which the students were on their own. I roused myself long enough for a single museum visit and met the students for a boat ride on the Seine. I knew that all I had left to do was get them on a plane heading west. Of course, that all fell apart, too. Upon arrival at Charles De Gaulle Airport, our flight, still 4 hours from departure, was overbooked. An unfriendly airline employee told me that they could take half the group at that moment and put them on an earlier flight that had enough empty seats to accommodate them. I stood there, once again, with 18 students looking at me, awaiting a decision. In my drug-addled state, the most important thing seemed to be to keep them all together where I could watch them. Chapin, sensing my impending breakdown, leaned over and said, "We've got it, Ace." I counted off eight of them and they quickly followed Chapin and the airline employee toward Security. The rest of them looked at me, still. "Stop looking at me!" I wanted to say. "I don't know what I'm doing!" Instead I said, "We'll all be home tonight. They'll just get to Atlanta a little ahead of us. We'll be on the same flight to Charlotte."

On the plane with half my group, I couldn't help imagining the other plane, with the rest of my students, small and vulnerable against the darkening western sky. They would arrive in Atlanta with time to spare for our connection to Charlotte. Our plane, delayed in Paris, would barely make it in time.

We touched down and headed for Customs, where the lines were long and hardly moving. I dug out my cell phone and prayed for a signal and battery power. I had both. I punched in Chapin's number, which he had pressed into my hand before he was whisked away to get on the earlier flight. "Chapin! We're here in Customs. Whatever you do, DO NOT LET THAT PLANE LEAVE WITHOUT US!"

"I'm all over it, Ace. Don't worry," he said nonchalantly. I hung up as my bag appeared on the carousel. I grabbed it and headed for the line. We got everyone through in fairly short order. I knew we had only about 10 minutes to get to a different terminal to board our flight to Charlotte, and with nine students in tow, nothing moved quickly. Alan and Tommy were with me and managed to herd the group along quickly. I called Chapin again.

"We're coming! Hold that plane!"

"Not a problem, Ace." Actually, as I found out a few minutes later, it was a problem. The plane had boarded, and only Chapin and Cannon were left at the gate.

The gate attendant looked extremely angry, and as I approached, I heard him say, "Get on or we're closing the door!" Chapin and Cannon were stalling, I realized. Cannon was tying his shoe, Chapin was digging in his bag. When they saw us coming, the relieved looks on their faces made me burst out laughing.

"Here we are," I said calmly to the gate attendant, as though this was a perfectly normal moment in my life. "Thanks for waiting." We filed through the door and onto the plane. I did one final headcount. Eighteen. I found my seat in the last row, sat down, looked out the window as the flight attendant lectured and the engines revved, and cried. Whether it was exhaustion, cold medicine, relief, or a combination of all three, that's what I did for the first 20 minutes of our short flight home: sobbed quietly to myself.

We parted for the final time at the terminal, each of us having secured our own rides home. My husband met me and gathered my bag while I stood with the group. "Hey, Ace," Alan said. "Want to know why we call you 'Ace'?"

"Um...I think so?"

"It stands for something." He looked around at the others who began laughing. "Ass Chewer Extraordinaire! That's you." With that, he grabbed his bag and followed the other Sweet Boys into the night, leaving me there to ponder the irony of such a moniker. Given the way I felt at that moment, "ass dragger" seemed more appropriate. I headed out of the terminal through a different door.

I didn't learn much French. I don't remember, years later, anything about the cathedrals or religious sites or even any of the restaurants. But I did learn, and always try to remember, this one thing: When everything's going wrong, and I can find neither a way out nor enough strength to climb one more step, I just need to look around for a group of students. The right ones, at the right time, in the right place, even a small town in France, will lift me up and carry me forward.

To My Mentor

Stan Carpenter

When I think about how to teach,
I remember how you taught me.
Broad in scope, sharp in detail,
Respectful of students and of ideas,
Past and future, seminal and possible.
I don't teach the same as you,
But my teaching started with you.

When I set out to write,
I remember how we wrote together.
Sharing and teaching and learning by turns, and
Now I know how precious was your gift of
Collaboration, and how difficult and rare.
I don't write the same as you,
But my writing started with you.

When I try to advise my students,
I remember how you advised me.
Listening and probing and challenging and seeking,
Not your path but my own, the best for me,
My own opinion, but with your knowledge and wisdom.
I don't advise the same as you,
But my advising started with you.

When I serve our profession,
I remember how you served and still serve.
Selflessly, tirelessly, continuously, diligently,
Involving all, but shouldering more than your share,
Distributing rewards, but accepting obligations personally.
I don't serve the same as you,
But my service started with you.

And when I try to think, to work through problems and
Theorize to fit the data and add to the store of knowledge,
I remember how you thought, with conversations and
Drafts and flowing ideas and excitement and passion.
And I value that most of all, for it's hard to replicate and rare, indeed.
I don't think the same as you,
But my thinking owes much to you.

I don't share all of your values
But I value all of your sharing.
Your example, your modeling, your inspiration
Are with me always,
And through me with others.
Your influence multiplied and altered,
Rippling through lives and minds.

For your work,
For your help,
For your time,
For your mentoring,
For your friendship,
For your example,
For your self—
Thank you.

WHAT GOES AROUND COMES AROUND: INSPIRATION IS CYCLICAL

JENNIFER O'CONNOR

As a former student affairs professional and a current professor of student affairs administration, I devote my professional work to helping students from working-class backgrounds succeed in higher education. By publishing and presenting at conferences, I do my best to educate the student affairs community about supporting first-generation college students and their special needs. My academic work is inspired by my personal journey.

Thirteen years ago, I was a working-class student at an Ivy League college. Scared and bewildered would be appropriate words to describe my emotions about the first day of orientation. Somehow I believed that—despite my top academic record, athletic accomplishments, and student government leadership positions—I had duped the admissions office. My father had not gone to college, and I, like many other first-generation college students, believed that I did not belong in the academic community.

I remember walking up the front steps to Converse Hall to meet administrators who were welcoming students. Upon those steps, I met Dean of Admissions Katie Fretwell and the woman who was about to become my student affairs mentor. She greeted me with warmth and a hug and said, "Jen O'Connor, we are so lucky to have you here. Amherst is going to be a better place the next 4 years because of you." I was shocked that the dean not only recalled my name, but remembered specific details about my application and how my essay statement about being the first in my family to attend college had left an indelible mark on her.

Despite Katie's reassurance, I hid my anxieties. I projected that I belonged at Amherst and that I knew what I was doing, so my privileged classmates accepted me. However, I hid my irrational insecurities, trying desperately to fit in despite my raggedy jeans and their designer clothes, my bus tickets home and their Jeep Cherokees, and my temporary jobs over breaks (to make money for the next semester's books) and their vacations to Hawaii.

However, throughout my 4 years, Katie was a source of unconditional support. During my sophomore year, she recruited me to join the student admissions staff. I enjoyed meeting prospective students and their families. My work in the admissions office became central to my college career. During my senior year, I helped plan and organize a welcoming day for accepted high school students. While leading the first tour of the day, I passed Katie on campus, and her message filled me with more delight than she could ever presume. She said, "Jen O'Connor, I can't imagine a better person to give the kick-off tour and welcome our prospectives." At this point in the tour, I approached the highest geographical point on campus—the big campus hill. Her comments in combination with the inner satisfaction I gained in welcoming students to campus made me feel as though I was standing on top of the hill, both literally and figuratively.

I sent Katie flowers the day I graduated from Amherst, and she responded by saying, "I should be the one sending you flowers." Words could not express the gratitude I felt toward her. She believed in me before I even arrived at Amherst and encouraged me throughout my 4 years. Anticipating a large paycheck, I accepted a corporate job after graduation. Katie said to me, "Congratulations, but to be honest, I really don't see you in the consulting world. I see you in education, higher education." Deep down, I knew she was right. Less than a year later, I called her to ask if she would be a reference for me as I applied to my first student affairs job in an admissions office.

A decade later, I prepare students to work in the field. Katie is still my close confidant and will always hold a special place in my heart. She was at my wedding, celebrated the birth of my first child, and remains a beloved personal and professional role model. Inspiration is truly a reciprocal process. Katie has revealed that a defining moment in her 20-plus-year career in student affairs was when she received an award as Outstanding

Mentor in the field of Student Affairs by a conglomeration of New England higher education associations. I nominated Katie for this award, and presenting it to her completed the cycle of mentor/mentee.

A decade ago, Katie and her staff supported the dreams of a first-generation college student. Today, I support the initiatives of Amherst College in recruiting more low-income students to campus.

KIMI'S LETTER

MATTHEW BIRNBAUM

A t the end of each semester, I sort through the many piles of paper around my office. One semester I rediscovered a single, coffee-stained sheet floating among the many stacks. Kimi, a first-year student I met when working in the career center, had sent me the note nearly 10 years ago. The note reminded me that a student affairs professional may never know how our well-intended efforts may ultimately influence the lives of students.

Kimi and I were in the process of sitting down in my office on a cold winter morning when she bluntly announced a desire to transfer. We were both getting comfortable in our chairs, and the speed with which she spoke felt rushed and artificial. The lack of pleasantries or introductory conversation left me defensive and scrambling to find an entry point for dialogue. In an attempt to start the conversation over, I asked Kimi about her winter break, but she just replied, "It was fine, but I really want to look into transferring."

Glancing at her intake form, I learned Kimi was from Hawaii, a long way from the snowy mountains of Colorado. My initial thought was that perhaps she was homesick. I told Kimi that I would be glad to assist but that it would be helpful if she could bring me up to speed on her decision. Perhaps sensing my need to more fully understand her situation, Kimi finally put down her backpack and settled into her chair.

Kimi's story resembled other, similar tales I had heard from other students about falling in love with the institution during their on-campus visit. Our university was located in a beautiful setting and radiated a feeling of community to all within earshot of the chapel's hourly chimes.

"The school is fine," Kimi said, "I'm having a great time here. But I wonder if there might be an institution that fits better with my image of the ideal college experience."

This was intriguing to me. Obviously Kimi had spent time reflecting upon the idea of what a college *should* be like and had not simply altered her image to fit what it actually was. This was not the type of student I wanted to transfer! Although this happened many years ago, I remember pressing Kimi to articulate her ideal college experience. "Well," she started several times, "it is really hard to put into words; they are more like feelings."

As we continued talking, my mind started wondering about Kimi's interest in transferring. Perhaps she had had a negative experience last semester. I leaned forward and asked her if something specific had happened. "No," she assured me. She stated that she appreciated and understood my concern, but that this was simply a matter of her thinking that there might be a school that better fit her idea of the ideal college. I was relieved by Kimi's response, but we were at an impasse. Kimi could not explain what type of experience she hoped to have at another institution, and I needed to understand why she wanted to transfer.

We both were frustrated. I asked Kimi if she would be willing to accept a short homework assignment, and she agreed without even asking what the assignment might involve. She responded to my question about as quickly as I had thought of it. Now I needed to think of an assignment. Just as I was about to suggest she start looking through some college review books, I noticed a *Fiske Guide* sticking out of her backpack. "Okay," I said, wondering what was about to come out of my mouth. "In one page, I want you to tell me what you want out of college."

"I can do that." Kimi said standing up. "This might help me come up with the words I am looking for. When do you want it?" "Never." I thought to myself, but instead smiled and said, "This is on your timeline; whenever you get to it." She agreed and left. It was possible that Kimi sensed my relief because she made it a point to assure me several times that the meeting was very helpful.

I saw Kimi walking through the student union a week later. We briefly made eye contact, and she simply smiled and continued a conversation with friends. "Well," I thought, "maybe she just needed time to readjust."

A week later Kimi came into my office gleaming, handed me a typed page, and said, "This was really helpful. Now I know what I am looking for." She turned and left for class. I glanced at the paper. It was thirteen bulleted sentences, each beginning with the words "I want." "I want, I want," I thought, "how self-centered. This is the kind of consumerism that drives me crazy." Then I read it more carefully:

WHAT DO I WANT OUT OF COLLEGE?

- I want a place where I feel like the intellectual challenge is what is important, where people identify me with what they know of my mind and of my soul, not with what they see of my ethnic background.

- I want college to be a place where those around me do not take this big privilege for granted. I know I do a lot of the time, but I want people my age to remind me of how lucky I am to be able to go to a school that costs so much.

- I want college to surround me with people who are serious about working, about playing, and about the balance between those two.

- I want a college to challenge who I am and who I am becoming, to push me through questioning me.

- I want college to show me what I can do and who I can be.

- I want college to be a sanctuary where I can explore extensively who I can be outside of academics.

- I want college to make me ready for the world I invent for myself. I want every professor to show me how good they are. I don't want to wonder why the college I go to gave tenure status to any of my professors. I want for college to amaze me with what the professors teach me and with how they present the material.

- I want college to make me feel that I am getting the best formal education I can get and that I am giving myself the best education I can give to myself. I want people to respect the hard work I put into my classes, for me not to feel like I have to defend the quality of education I am getting.

- I want college to be a home I bask in, where I feel and believe I belong.

- I want college to encourage me to grow personally and emotionally. I want my college to make me really believe, to convince me, that the place has offered me everything college has to offer.

- I want college to help me be more opened-minded and more giving. I want for college to help me to be a better person, to be more of who I want to be.

- I want college to keep my mind alive and to prod it to flourish, even as other influences encourage me to believe that an intellectual, academic life has little or no value.

- I want college to energize and invigorate me, to show me all the ways I can use my experiences, to show me how to live a full life in the world I will enter after these few short years are done, in the common sense of college being done.

I reread each sentence, taking in the meaning. While each focused on something Kimi wanted from her college, they did not indicate that she wanted a consumerist, banking-like relationship with her alma mater. Instead, she described wanting a profound and deeply engaging relationship with the college and her fellow students. I wish I could tell the reader that Kimi and I engaged in numerous follow-up conversations, but the truth of the matter is that I never saw her again! She never came back to the career center, our paths never crossed in the student union, and soon she no longer was enrolled.

A year after our meeting, I came across Kimi's letter. On a whim, I made a photocopy and mailed the original to her home address with a short note stating that I hoped she was having her idealized college experience. I like to think that Kimi received the letter and took a minute to reflect on her words and decision. For my part, Kimi's letter reminds me that we rarely know how our work and interactions, no matter how fleeting, may affect a college student.

Ignorance Is Not Bliss

Joy Hoffman

During the first part of my career, I worked at a small, private university; a predominantly White, faith-based institution. I was the director of student leadership, primarily responsible for student government, new-student orientation, student activities, and large-scale programming. Of the 75 students under my advisement, the number of students of color involved in leadership never exceeded 10 during any given year. In the 7 years I worked there, only two students of color ever served on an executive board. Further, students of color served primarily in cultural organizations or student groups that represented minority populations.

As I reflect on this experience, I am hesitant to admit that I saw no problem with this, nor did I intentionally recruit students of color to serve in influential positions. I am not suggesting that cultural organizations are not influential, but executive boards and students in other positions always had more of a voice. They were heard while others were tolerated, misunderstood, or silenced.

I enjoyed the comfortable world I lived and worked in, where race was not an issue and everyone had the same opportunities. No one was treated differently, or so I thought. Then I met Linda. She was a Black student who was referred to me by a colleague because she was looking for a job on campus. I hired her as an office assistant and thus began an incredible journey. She and her friends would frequently visit even when not working, and we would chat about current issues, classes, life experiences, and campus climate. My eyes were opened. I clearly remember Linda venting about a news story that highlighted the anniversary of the Columbine shootings. She noted that when Columbine occurred, the news buzzed for weeks and people "wondered how any of this could happen." She mourned friends in her community who had been shot due to gang violence, but no one knew about them because their stories did not matter. I will never forget an insight she shared. "They expect it in our community," she said. "They think that's just the way we [Blacks] are, so it is not news. They would never give this much attention to my neighborhood. We lose kids every day to shootings. It's not because we're Black; it's because we are invisible." I could only listen and encourage, but when I got home, I cried. This brief conversation became a turning point in my career. Quite literally, it changed my life.

By choice, I began co-coordinating programs with the intercultural office, which was staffed by a part-time graduate student. Together we established the first cross-cultural fair on campus and offered town hall meetings, cross-cultural events, and diversity retreats for students to attend. Although I enjoyed working in orientation, student activities, and student government, my new passion was directing me elsewhere. Within 2 years, I sought jobs that focused on diversity and social justice.

After 7 years in multicultural services, I am often perceived as an expert in my field. I facilitate retreats and workshops, present at conferences, teach classes, and consult through leadership positions and committees. On the outside, I display a confidence that is very convincing. But in the deepest places in my soul, I wish I could repent ignorant behavior, tasteless jokes, and oppressive language. I long to find the people I've hurt in the past and say "I'm sorry." I want to tell them that I've changed, that I am an ally, and that I have committed my life to social justice. Then I realize how selfish that is, because their pain has nothing to do with what I think I have accomplished. I hide behind my confidence and professionalism as a person who mourns past transgressions and still has so much to learn.

Daily life continues to educate me. Students share their perspectives. Colleagues enlighten me with new insights and discoveries. Personal experiences challenge me to think inclusively and compassionately. I am passionate, but also patient. I ask for forgiveness and must remember to forgive. I teach, advocate, and challenge. I continue to ask questions. Yes, I still suffer from ignorance. I appreciate those who walk alongside me so we can learn from each other. Truth be told, I would have nothing to teach today if a student had not taught me one of the most important lessons of my career. Thank you, Linda.

KEBBA

LAURA THOMPSON

I have worked with college students since 1994. During this time, I've held numerous titles and roles in a multitude of settings. The students I've met along the way come from diverse cultural and socioeconomic backgrounds, and they have ranged in terms of aptitude, motivation levels, and future aspirations. Many of them have entertained me and made me laugh. A few have frustrated me and made me cry. Some have stimulated me intellectually, while others have challenged me to wonder why I chose this particular career path. Thankfully, there have been students who have motivated and inspired me to be a better person. I would like to tell you the story of one of these students. His name is Kebba.

Kebba has a childlike purity and sweetness about him that lights up a room. There is a stillness and knowing about him that exudes wisdom beyond his years. His giggle is precious and contagious. I can't help but smile when I see him.

I first met Kebba 3 years ago when he began attending Franklin College, a small American-accredited school in Switzerland, where I work. It was my first year at Franklin, too. When Kebba arrived from The Gambia, everyone was worried about how he would adapt. He seemed painfully shy and spent much of his time alone in his room. Would this experience prove to be too much for him? Had we set our expectations too high? Was bringing him here the right decision? Whether people at Franklin would admit it or not, I knew they were concerned about his ability to succeed. Deep down, I believe we were afraid. We were afraid that he might fail or, even worse, that we might fail him.

As the fall semester got under way, Kebba slowly started to come out of his shell. His love of soccer and skill on the field quickly helped him win friends among the other members of the men's soccer team. He seemed to be doing quite well navigating his cultural adjustment, yet none of us could truly comprehend what he was experiencing. We didn't know anything about his past or all he had been through to get to this place.

At some point in that first semester, Kebba wasn't feeling well. Our school nurse wasn't able to stay at the hospital, so I went to be with him. As we sat there in the waiting room, Kebba told me about his life. He was born in Senegal and lived there with his family until he was about 5 years old. His parents and siblings were captured by rebels. For some reason, Kebba was spared. He was too young and too little to be a child soldier. He wasn't strong enough to hold a gun.

At this time, his grandmother took him with her to live in The Gambia. He lived with her until she died. He was 13. Kebba now had nowhere to live, and he had to find a way to pay for his schooling. He tried to get help from government agencies, but he was not successful. Benefits usually went to Gambians first. He ended up selling the furniture from the apartment his grandmother rented so that he could pay tuition for another year. Kebba slept in different places, frequently in mosques.

The next year, Kebba dropped out of school because he didn't have enough money for tuition. During this year, he did some work for other people, and then he was able to persuade the administration of his school to allow him to return. They let him skip a grade, and he went on to finish his last year.

Around the time his grandmother died, Kebba started to write letters asking people for support. "It was like a voice inside told me to write," he said. "I wrote letters like crazy!" He said there were several hotels in the area where he lived. He would go to their trash to find discarded newspapers and magazines. He would scour these materials for addresses. He would sell vegetables that he grew on a small plot of land to buy stamps. For 4 or 5 years, Kebba wrote letters.

At one point, he came across a brochure for Franklin College. Inside, the names and addresses of members of the board of trustees were printed. Kebba wrote to everyone on the list. This is how his relationship with Franklin College began. Months later, he received a response from one of the board members. Kebba and this particular board member wrote letters back and forth over the course of several years. In the meantime, Kebba got a scholarship to attend a hotel school in The Gambia. The trustee wanted to see how Kebba would do. He told Kebba that when he finished, if he was still interested in coming to Franklin to pursue a degree, he would help him. He did.

As I sat there in the waiting room, I was amazed and touched by Kebba's story. It was one of those moments in life where I was overcome by a profound sense of clarity and perspective. How is it that my life had been so easy by comparison? It certainly didn't seem fair.

As the Christmas holiday approached, Kebba prepared himself to go back to The Gambia for the break. When he returned to Switzerland, he had more health problems. He couldn't sleep, and he began having terrible headaches and nightmares. He was convinced that someone had put a black magic spell on him while he was in Africa. As a devout Muslim, he admitted that the practice of black magic was something he had never believed in before these health problems began. While an initial reaction from a western mind might be "this kid needs a psychiatrist," after talking with him at great length, it was clear that he was approaching this problem from a mentally sound place.

Could it be stress from adjusting to a new place? *Maybe.* Could it be a manifestation of guilt caused by having grown up as an orphan in poverty and having been given the privilege to study at a very expensive school in Switzerland? *Perhaps.* The bottom line, however, was that for him, the experience was very real. In his culture, black magic was something that was practiced. Helping him wasn't so much about finding a western solution to a problem with very nonwestern roots, but rather finding a solution that made sense for him in the context of his culture. Kebba had several meetings with a psychologist to talk about culture shock; in the meantime, I spent a lot of time researching black magic and contacted people who might know something about it. Through several connections, I found someone who had a practice of breaking spells. I connected Kebba with this person. In the end, I'm not sure which intervention was the most effective, but I knew that he was better, and our bond was closer because of that experience.

With each year, it has been gratifying to watch Kebba. He's more sure of himself now. He understands the way things work on campus, and he seems more willing to seek assistance.

Last spring, Kebba came into my office and sat down. "Laura," he said in his thick accent. "The thing is, I kind of have this problem." He smiled sheepishly, and I listened. "You see, I don't know how old I am, and I would like to know. I know that the age in my documents is wrong. It says that I am older than I actually am." I imagined what it would be like not to know how old I am or my birthday. He explained to me that for him to be eligible for the scholarship for hotel school, he needed to be a particular age. As he wasn't a Gambian native, it was already quite difficult for him to compete for this award. His school counselor had changed his age on his records so he would be eligible for this opportunity.

"Well," I said, "this is certainly a unique problem." I asked him if perhaps he might be able to get a birth certificate from Senegal. He was pretty sure that such a thing didn't exist in the village where he was born. I pondered possible options. I called a friend of mine who teaches biology. "How exactly would one go about finding out how old one is?" I asked. I know my friend thought I had lost it. He explained that forensic scientists often look at teeth to determine age. "Yes," I said, "but this person isn't dead." We laughed, and Kebba laughed too. We still don't know his age.

When I think about Kebba's story, I think of a million reasons why he could be someone so different today. He could be unhappy, or bitter, resentful, and angry at the world. He's not. He's just kind, gentle, and good. His story has challenged me on many levels and has reminded me about what is truly important in life. Kebba has provided me with a gratifying sense of purpose and richness in my work. In May, Kebba will graduate from Franklin College. This is a day that I have looked forward to for a very long time.

Over Your Shoulder

David DiElsi

P aul, a student I once tutored, came from the inner city. Our meetings occurred in the midst of a busy learning lab where other students came and went for tutoring sessions. Paul and I had a few sessions together, but I didn't seem to be getting through to him. He seemed constantly distracted, alert to every sound and diverted by anyone who entered the room or passed by.

He was certainly bright enough to perform the work, but he wasn't attending to it very well. Finally, I described his behavior to him and said something like, "Just ignore all the stuff going on around us and focus on our work." He replied, "Dave, where I come from, if you don't know exactly who and what is going on around you at all times, you could get shot." That stunned me into the realization that personal security is something I take for granted. This student didn't feel safe—even in a relatively secure environment. From then on, I adjusted our position during the sessions so Paul would have no one moving behind him and a clear view of the entrance and the rest of the room. Although he continued to constantly check on what was happening around us, I no longer interpreted that action as a sign of inattention or boredom.

I wondered how many other times I incorrectly assumed that I knew what was behind students' behavior. I began to think of students' actions as driven by circumstances not necessarily connected to the academic activity of the moment. Now, I try to reach students in the presence of their own approach to the material, instead of trying to change their approach into what I think it should be. This insight has made me more versatile in my work and has helped students dramatically increase the productivity of their tutoring sessions.

The Big Panty Raid

Jacqueline Cooper

As student affairs professionals, we often find ourselves personally dealing with transition issues, just like the students and parents we serve. As we move from place to place, we transition to new living environments and learn the formal and informal rules of our new colleagues and institutions. During the hustle and bustle of the academic year, we often forget that we sometimes act like students. Here's a story of the antics at new-student orientation.

Not only was I the new kid on the block, I was the new kid in the state. This translated to making many major transitions, including leaving the Midwest snow and coming to never-ending, unforgiving, unrelenting, and just plain nasty summer heat.

I arrived on campus armed with student development theories, a couple of management theories, years of experience gained from working with residential summer programs, and my almost completed PhD.

My new orientation team was motivated and prepared. Despite the cruel heat, I knew I had made the right decision. I became orientation!

Graduate school taught me that I should conduct environmental scans on my new job. In other words, I needed to take a close look at everything so I could find areas for improvement. My scan identified that my new orientation team thrived on rituals and traditions. I learned about the Happy Box, the Unhappy Box, and the Secret Pal tradition, to name a few. However, there was a really big tradition that was unknown to me.

It was the second day of a 2-day freshmen session. Early that day, my boss told me that she was coming by later to say hi to the team. "No problem." I said. I quickly added, "I am sure the team will enjoy seeing you." If only I knew.

When the last of the 600 students and parents completed class registration and no one was sitting in lost and found, my student coordinators and I prepared for our wrap-up meeting. The general agenda included (1) a reality check on the session, and (2) greetings from my boss to the team.

Around 4:00 p.m. the team started to gather for the wrap-up meeting in the lobby of the residence hall we called home for the summer. Ding! Team members step off the elevator. My boss and I stood near the lobby chairs, patiently waiting. Ding! The elevator signaled its arrival again. More team members step off the elevator. However, they looked a little different. The newly arriving team members, all young men, stepped off the elevator wearing several pairs of panties on their heads! Some of the guys completed their look by draping bras over their shoulders while other guys sported dangling bras from their arms! We were in the middle of a panty raid! I felt the blood leave my face. For one of the few times in my life, I was speechless. I looked at my boss. Oh no! She looked worse than I did. She stood straight, arms crossed. Her posture proved a visual testament to her stoic personality and her Midwestern reserve.

My boss and I did what grown folk of a certain age and with some level of responsibility generally do during times like these: We stood and watched. The rest of the assembled student team reacted very differently. They hooted in laughter and cheered as the guys calmly strolled across the lobby proudly displaying the spoils of their plunder. We all watched as the guys savored every triumphant moment.

Ding! The elevator arrived again. All heads snapped in its direction. Some very discontented and unhappy-looking young ladies stepped off the elevator. From the scowls on their faces, they had to be the owners of said underwear now on proud public display in the lobby. The young ladies' eyes raced around the room as they did their own scanning. They quickly located the guilty panty stealers. The guys strolled around layered in panties and bras, providing quite an explosion of colors, styles, fabrics, and designs. As panty stealers go, they were true champs.

Like lionesses on the prowl, the young ladies quickly leaped into action. They proceeded to chase the guys. However, unlike lionesses that chase their prey with stealth and silence, the young ladies pursued the guys yelling and screaming at the top of their lungs as they raced around the lobby. When the young ladies caught the guys, they quickly recovered their underwear. To add more to the situation, the young ladies even landed a few punches in the process.

With the underwear back in their possession, the young ladies marched back to the elevators. This event happened very quickly. However, it felt like an eternity. My boss was still standing stiff beside me. I was supposed to be supervising this team. I could only imagine what was going though her mind. When I found my voice, I could only say, "Wow!" My boss said, "That was interesting." "Yeah, they like to play," I added. Then it happened. I burst out laughing. The panty raid was truly funny.

When the brooding young ladies came back downstairs, they found that the panty-raiding guys were still laughing and reveling in the fact that they had successfully pulled off the prank. That's right. My boss and I witnessed a display of the most sacred tradition held by orientation teams: They lived for pranks! Pranks were not only fun for them and provided an outlet for them to express their creativity, this tradition helped bond and strengthen the team.

I later learned that what we witnessed was actually part two of the prank. The owners of the underwear had started the prank a couple days earlier. The young ladies had a reputation of being "prank masters." According to the story, the ladies had gone into several of the men's rooms and taken their clothes from their closets. After the guys discovered that their clothes were missing, they decided payback was in order—and the payback had to be big. The guys had upped the ante and staged the big panty raid in the residence hall lobby in the presence of the entire team!

The very nature of a prank is to out-prank other pranksters. With this prank, the men reigned supreme. In fact, the big panty raid remained the top prank for the entire summer.

My boss eventually recovered. Over the years and even through her stoicism, she eventually gained the ability to laugh about the prank. The lesson? Learning is a big part of transitioning. Learning new traditions on new jobs is a part of transitioning. The best way to learn a tradition is to not have it told to you. Rather, you should experience the tradition first hand, panty raids and all!

The Accidental Educator

Ronni Sanlo

The Unintended Path

It was not my envisioned career path to become a student affairs professional or the lesbian-in-charge on a college campus. I was the "princess" from Miami Beach, and I wanted to be a rabbi. Back then, in the early 1960s, I was told that all I could hope to be was a rabbi's wife. I went to the University of Florida, where my father said I should work to obtain my Mrs. degree. He meant that I should find a husband. I was a music major and intended to become a high school band director. I married one instead.

At 31, I came out as a lesbian, having spent 20 very painful years in the sick silence of the closet. I lost custody of my two very young children when I came out, which created a different kind of pain, one that was filled with and fueled by intense anger at the injustice. I became a wild and risk-taking activist, until I finally fell into exhaustion from the anger that guided my life.

My career path took a number of twists and turns. I was fired from many jobs in Florida in those early years because of my sexual orientation. I eventually found my way to working with people with AIDS, a very unpopular but desperately needed task in the mid-1980s. The pay was minimal, but the benefits included continuing education. I earned a master's degree and then a doctorate in education. It still astounds me that the state that took my children away from me provided me with free graduate education!

In 1994, because of my history of LGBT street activism, my organizing skills, and my degrees, I was hired by the University of Michigan to direct its Office of Lesbian, Gay, Bisexual, and Transgender Affairs. I became a new professional in student affairs at the age of 47. This is where my stories begin.

During my first month at Michigan, I was called by a nurse to come to the hospital because a student patient wanted to talk with me. He had seen the article about me in the school paper a week earlier, so he knew my name. When I entered his room, I saw a pale young man lying in bed, covers pulled up to his mouth. He looked as if he were 10 years old. I walked over to his side and took his hand.

"Hi," I said softly. "I'm Ronni."

"Hi, Dr. Ronni," he said in such a quiet small voice. "My name's Richard. I'm a sophomore and I'm president of my fraternity, or I was until I tried to kill myself." He took a deep breath. "I read about you in the paper. I need to talk to someone who will understand."

"What would you like me to understand, Richard?" I asked.

After another deep breath and with tears welling up in his deep blue eyes, Richard said, "I'm gay. God, I've never said that before. I'm gay. I've been living in a horrible hell of secrets and silence. I feel so alone. It just hurts my heart. I tried to stop the pain by stopping me." He was in the hospital because his suicide attempt, thank goodness, failed.

His parents were on their way. Richard was petrified, although he had asked them to come. Richard's father was a retired military officer and former football player. His mother was an elected official in the conservative town where they lived. They were Republican and Catholic. Richard kept saying, "They'll hate me. I know it. I'm such a disappointment to them. I can't bear that." He cried. He talked. I listened, witnessing both his pain and his strength as he mustered some confidence.

Richard's parents arrived, both tall, attractive, obviously powerful people. Richard's mother ran to him, held him, said very little through her tears. She made way for his father, a large man who appeared to be in nearly as much emotional pain as his son. In a soft and gentle voice unusual for a man his size, he asked his son, "What's going on?" Through his tears, the young man said, "Dad, I'm gay, and I don't want to embarrass or shame you and Mom." The big man gently scooped his son up in his arms and, incredibly and unexpectedly, said to him, "Son, if you're gay, you get out of this bed and be the best damn gay man you can be."

Richard graduated two years later. He was accepted to law school and is a successful attorney today. Richard dedicated his undergraduate honors thesis to me. That cherished manuscript is in my office as a reminder of that young man's courage—and the courage of so many of our students—to survive.

THE NIGHT MINDY DIED

I remember the night Mindy died. I was with her earlier that evening. We attended a film screening on campus, then walked back to our residence hall together. I was a faculty-in-residence in the hall where Mindy lived. She often came to my apartment to study in the quiet of my space or to talk about the issues that affected her on any given day, including her depression.

Mindy was one of those special students for me. You know the kind—the one who inadvertently makes her or his way into your office before you even know they're there, and then you want to adopt them. While I felt quite connected to many of my students time after time, there was always that one special child who reminds me why I do this student affairs work. Mindy was such a student for me.

I first met Mindy when I was the faculty guinea pig—I mean chaperone—on a camping trip hosted by our Recreation Department's Outdoor Adventures program for new students. Twelve first-year students, three Outdoor Adventures staff, and this old Jewish dyke who hates camping went on a 3-day camping and kayaking trip. I noticed Mindy right away. She reminded me of a thousand young lesbians with whom I'd worked over the years. Mindy wasn't out to anyone yet, so she avoided me, until I took her to the airport when the camping trip concluded. In my car for the 90-minute ride, she chatted incessantly about my ineptness as a camper. I responded with, "Hey! I'm Jewish and I'm old. I need the Sheraton!" But Mindy cut me no slack. She hopped out of the car at the terminal and was gone. Poof! Just like that. School wouldn't start for another month.

During move-in several weeks later, as the new school year was about to begin, there was a knock on my apartment door. "Hi, Dr. Ronni. Remember me?" From that moment on, Mindy was a frequent visitor. She came to my office or my apartment, most often when she felt depressed or was excited. It didn't occur to me yet that Mindy might be cycling through the ups and downs of mental illness.

During those times when she said she felt depressed, Mindy's face would become pale, all color gone from her cheeks and lips, and she would become afraid of herself. During her upswings, she would often seek quiet places that didn't feel like sensory overload. I realized that's when I saw her most often, when she was cycling up. I connected her with a therapist in our student counseling center, but Mindy had her secrets that she wouldn't share with the therapist or with me.

Mindy was an outstanding student despite having the reputation in the residence hall as a party girl. As well as I knew her, I had no idea that she played—and drank—with gusto. Regardless, Mindy was adored by everyone with whom she came into contact. By the start of her sophomore year, she had come out to her parents and friends as a lesbian, had a crush on a new girlfriend whom she planned to visit over the winter break, and had been accepted into the study abroad program for the following year. In January she would begin the LGBT studies minor, about which she was very excited. It was almost Thanksgiving, and she was looking forward to flying home the following week for both the holiday and her father's birthday.

I was training for the Honolulu marathon with the National AIDS Marathon Training Program. The final 22-mile training run was on Sunday, November 14, 2004. I asked my residence hall students to be volunteers at the water stops for the runners. Mindy volunteered and showed up at 5:30 a.m. for the first shift, but she stayed the entire day. She said it was one of the most meaningful things she'd ever done because it was helping people with AIDS. She cheered me on mightily as I ran by her station.

The following Thursday evening, November 18, Mindy and I met at an on-campus theater to see a film and to hear a discussion by the director and actors. We walked back to our residence hall together around 10 p.m. Mindy seemed to be in good spirits. I asked her what she was going to do now. She said she was working on an outline that was due in the morning. I hugged her goodnight and went to my apartment to work on an article.

As I sat at my desk near my living room window, I saw the lights of the emergency vehicles, too many vehicles for the occasional drunk student lying in the grass. I went into the hallway to see what was going on. It was quiet on my floor, so I went up to the next. I could see the resident assistant, my sweet friend Chris, down the hall, running toward me. He stopped in front of me, a look of horror on his face, tears landing on his shirt. He put his arms around me, sobbing. "Dr. Ronni, It's Mindy." I knew.

I miss Mindy. I am no longer angry with her for leaving me and her friends and her parents, who will grieve for their only child for the rest of their lives. I still see her face in the nooks and crannies of the residence hall and campus. Strangely, the gifts I've received as a result of this unspeakable tragedy are many, and I feel so blessed. Because of Mindy, I've allowed myself to open my heart to students whom I never would have met, to be more real with them, and to have the courage to ask the hard questions of them if I have a concern. I keep the memory of Mindy close to me like a cherished old friend, and her beloved Frisbee hangs in my office, reminding me to celebrate every student who enters my space.

NEVER GIVE UP

"Ronni, there's no money or glory in master's programs, so forget it." I won't tell you which well-known researcher in student affairs said those words to me. I don't give up easily. If I did, I'd probably still be getting fired from mindless jobs in Florida. My graduate intern and I did some research and wrote the initial proposal to establish a master's in student affairs at the University of California at Los Angeles. The proposal was accepted, a design team was established, and the UCLA MEd in student affairs was approved. Today I am the program director. I was made a clinical professor.

Working in a graduate-preparation program is important to me. It is casting the net wider than just doing the work myself as a practitioner. I could certainly continue to do LGBT work, but if I teach new professionals about social justice and diversity that includes LGBT students and their issues, I will have a broader impact on our profession. More important, the impact will be felt with a variety of student populations.

I feel that my LGBT work has reached its full potential. While I had no contact with my own children for many years, I have had the privilege of working with other people's children for periods of time. I was on a mission to create a safer world for LGBT youth. When my own son came out as a gay man with his sanity and self-esteem intact, I knew I had done my job well.

Today I have the privilege of working with graduate students. While I still love my LGBT work, especially as an author, the actual hands-on campus work in student affairs now belongs to the next generation. New professionals with courage and dreams will take this work further than I could ever imagine. They will not be hampered by lavender ceilings and antiquated laws. They will turn the safe paths into social justice superhighways.

I have been very blessed in this great career path. It is not the path I planned, not by a long shot. But as a woman, a mother, a grandmother; as one who keeps students at the center of my focus, I cannot imagine working in any field other than higher education. It took me 47 years to find this profession—although I know that the profession found me— and I am deeply grateful.

In Four Days

James D. Hardwick

"Either you've just had a major heart attack, or you have a virus on your heart, or you are just about to have a major attack," the doctor told me grimly. "I would bet on the virus on the heart."

As the dean of students, I had 2 more days of summer orientation to host that week before I started a 3-week leave to begin classes for my doctoral program. I did not have time to contemplate a major heart attack or a virus on my heart.

"I would like to send you over to the hospital to have an echocardiogram done," the doctor explained. "I would like to have a cardiologist view the echo before I hospitalize you."

I started to mentally tick off the phone calls I would need to make when I arrived at the office. I needed to alert my staff and coworkers that I might need their help to cover my responsibilities for the last session of summer orientation. Looking back, I am amazed how work-focused I was when the doctor was trying to communicate life-threatening news to me. As if he read my mind, the doctor began to articulate his expectations for my day until we knew the results of the echocardiogram.

"You are not going to the office today. You are going to go home to lie quietly on the couch until you receive my phone call," he said as sternly as possible. "Promise me that you will call an ambulance if you feel any pain or tightness in your chest."

I promised that I would call an ambulance. I started to make a mental list of family and friends to call as soon as I knew the results of the echo. I drove to the hospital on autopilot, running through the summer orientation schedule and mentally reassigning my responsibilities to coworkers. I had the echocardiogram done at the hospital and went home to lie on the couch waiting for the news. The cardiologist confirmed my doctor's suspicion. I was relieved to learn from my doctor—given the three options he had outlined for me in his exam room—that I had a virus on my heart, which had caused my heart to enlarge in my chest.

How ironic would it be for me to die from being big-hearted, I thought to myself. I contemplated the field day my coworkers would have with this diagnosis. I wondered how many other student affairs professionals secretly died from being big-hearted. More than we would like to admit.

The doctor gave me an early morning appointment to meet with the cardiologist to discuss the enlarged heart. He made me promise again that I would call an ambulance if I felt any tightness in my chest, any pain in my left arm, or any pain along my jaw. When the doctor called me at home 4 hours later to see how I was feeling, I could hear the concern in his voice. I asked the doctor what was bothering him, and he expressed concern as to whether he should hospitalize me rather than allow me to stay at home that night. I asked him point-blank if he wanted me to check into the hospital. After serious consideration, he decided to wait until after my early morning meeting with the cardiologist.

The next morning, I went to the cardiologist's office instead of to the first day of the 2-day summer orientation session. The cardiologist gave the enlarged heart an official name: cardiomyopathy. Despite all of my conversations with my doctor the night before about being hospitalized, I was stunned when he told me that I was going to be checked into a cardiac monitoring unit for the next 4 days. The cardiologist explained that my trip to the cardiac monitoring unit was a precaution as I started on medications to protect my heart and help the virus clear my system.

Thinking about my doctoral program that was starting in 4 days, I asked about restrictions after I checked out of the cardiac monitoring unit. The cardiologist told me that I could expect to be home from work for the next month and that I would need to take it easy for the next 3 months.

"You can take a calendar and count out 90 days from today," the cardiologist explained. "Circle the date on your calendar. If the medications do what they are supposed to do, you will feel like a cat climbed off of your chest when you reach that date on your calendar. The heart will not be completely back to its original size, but it will be significantly smaller than it is now."

I waited as long as I could. I asked the cardiologist if I would be able to attend classes during the first month away from work. I had a 3-week leave planned from work. I would be in class from 8 a.m. until noon and from 1 p.m. until 5 p.m., Monday through Friday. The classes ran for only 3 weeks. I remember the cardiologist looking at me skeptically and asking how stressful starting a doctoral program would be.

"Stress? There's no stress," I replied. "Going to class will actually be a vacation from work."

The cardiologist reluctantly agreed that I could start my program, but I would have to start classes 1 day late. He was unwilling to compromise on the 4 days that he wanted me in the cardiac monitoring unit. He also had one more restriction that I would have to fit into my class schedule.

"After each meal, you are going to have to lie down for 1 hour after you eat. Given the inefficiencies of your enlarged heart, you will have less oxygen in your system. Your body is going to need oxygen to digest your food. You will be too lightheaded for the first hour after lunch to be able to sit up in class. You will have to lie down on the floor."

The cardiologist left the exam room, and a nurse appeared to escort me down the hall to the cardiac monitoring unit in the hospital. Surprised at the suddenness of the check-in, I asked if I could take a few hours to make a few phone calls and to pack an overnight bag. The nurse smiled and told me that I was checking into the hospital now.

A few minutes later, I was in a backless hospital gown with an IV attached to my wrist, hearing instructions about my next 4 days. I quickly realized that I had become the talk of the cardiac monitoring unit—none of the nurses could recall someone as young as 37 years old being in their unit. Most of their patients, they explained, were in their 60s or 70s. I spent the rest of the afternoon assuring the nurses on shift that the birthdate on my patient chart was correct. When my doctor visited me during his rounds in the hospital, he explained the curiosity of my presence in the cardiac monitoring unit.

"Cardiomyopathy has no symptoms or warning signs. The virus settles into the heart, and the heart starts to work inefficiently. The heart muscle overcompensates and begins to overwork, causing the heart to enlarge in the chest cavity. Given the fact that there are no warning signs, most patients with cardiomyopathy have their heart explode inside their chest. You could be standing in the lobby of this hospital, have your heart explode, and the best heart surgeons in the world would likely not be able to save you. The nurses in the cardiac monitoring unit don't see many patients with enlarged hearts because the condition is rarely caught in time." He paused to let me absorb the information he shared.

"So tell me: I know how much you hate coming in for doctor appointments. What made you call for an appointment and come to the office to see me?"

Having heard his description of no symptoms and no warning signs, I know he was looking for some insight from a patient whose heart had not exploded. Unfortunately, I had nothing to give him.

"I had a feeling that something was wrong," I replied. I acknowledged that I could not recall any symptoms that caused me concern. I simply called the doctor's office as soon as they opened and told the receptionist I had a concern about my heart. The doctor knew as well as I did that while I had not had any previous heart concerns, I had reported cardiac problems in my family tree.

Not surprisingly, the last session of summer orientation went well without me. I called the faculty coordinator for the doctoral program and explained that I had an enlarged heart. I asked for permission to start my classes 1 day late and to be able to lie down on the classroom floor for the first hour after lunch for this first 3-week session of classes.

After 4 days, I left the cardiac monitoring unit with a feeling that I had cheated death. I recognized all the noise I carried around inside myself. I saw how many times I compromised my presence and peace of mind as a student affairs professional by mentally clicking through my things-to-do list for the day, the week, and the month. I found the silence in the cardiac monitoring unit to be deafening. With the 3-week leave from work for my doctoral classes extended to 4 weeks away from the office, I had no need to mentally review lists. I learned to live in the moment.

I was plagued by one nagging question: What if I had not listened to my instincts and had not called the doctor's office for an appointment? What if the noise inside me—obsessing about what needed to be done next in my student affairs position—had drowned out the voice that told me something was wrong?

In 4 days in the cardiac monitoring unit, I became a better student affairs professional. While I had always had a "calm in a crisis" reputation in my work as a dean of students, I developed an inner peace as a person and as a professional after listening to myself for 4 days. The introduction of an inner calmness in my life and work marked a critical life change for me. The calmness helped me through my doctoral program, an unexpected change in employment, and a relocation that has been personally and professionally rewarding.

In the 10 years since this cardiomyopathy episode, I have repeatedly revisited the question of how many student affairs professionals are killing themselves by being too big-hearted. I have challenged student affairs colleagues to flex their work schedules, to set reasonable expectations for their work goals, and to periodically take a few days—maybe 4 days—as a break from their student affairs responsibilities. I did not want to have any big-hearted student affairs professionals die on my watch. After all, when it comes to an enlarged heart, there are no symptoms and no warning signs.

Access or Excess?

Linda Gillingham

If there's one thing that we as advisors all have in common, it is accessibility to students. We do workshops in multiple and miscellaneous locations across campus. We advise in offices, corridors, classrooms, and university centers. When we're called upon to do so by professors, we jump at the chance to speak to classes. Our aim is to reach our students any way possible, almost anywhere, anytime. This is our mantra, and we are committed to it! That being said, let me illustrate just how effectively I have convinced students of this accessibility factor.

Shopping at Meijer (the midwestern equivalent of a Super Wal-Mart) at 5:30 p.m. on a weekday is a real experience. From craziness in the parking lot to hungry shoppers hurrying to pick up dinner items, the frenzied pace is not exactly the ideal environment in which to unwind after a busy day of student service. When you don't plan ahead, you have to pay the price. On this particular day, every aisle was crowded, and my number at the deli was 181. I contemplated how long it would be before I could put dinner on the table.

Finally, with deli items and groceries in tow, I attempted to find the shortest checkout line. I found myself #4 behind one man with a single item and two organized drivers of sparsely filled carts. After several minutes, I approached the grocery belt and unloaded my items, noticing that the line behind me had lengthened considerably. I smiled at Nora, the cashier, and we exchanged a comment or two about the weather. Our forecast predictions, however, were cut short by the ringing of the phone next to the cash register. As Nora answered the phone, she turned to me with a quizzical look and asked, "Are you Linda Gillingham?" I cautiously nodded my head while thinking, "Oh, my, something must be wrong at home, and my kids are trying to find me!" Judging from the impatient looks on their faces, however, the owners of the five carts behind me in line were not as concerned by the call.

I took the phone, and all eyes were now on the strange lady who gets phone calls at the Meijer checkout. As I said "Hello," a loud excited voice startled me with, "I am so bummed. I'm not going to graduate until a year from this May!" Holding the phone away from my ear, I said to Nora in a hushed voice, "Who IS this?" She pointed down about eight lanes, and I suddenly saw the checkout person in lane #17 frantically waving me down from her cash register. I slowly waved and smiled as inconspicuously as possible and turned back to the phone. While I was tempted to say, "Take two aspirin and call me in the morning," I said brightly, "Let's get together and talk about your plans. Why don't you call me first thing in the morning to set up a time?" As the "conversation" ended, I casually handed the puzzled Nora the phone, took my receipt, loaded my bags in the cart, and strolled out the door.

After the embarrassment of all this attention wore off, I realized that perhaps I had been promoting the idea of accessibility—anywhere, anytime—a little too enthusiastically. Sure makes a good story at advisor get-togethers, though!

EATING HUMBLE PIE

JENNIFER O'CONNOR

Today I might be a professor of student affairs administration, but I think it's important to share my humble career beginnings.

Many of the students in my graduate classes feel frustrated when beginning their first job search. As undergraduates, they were student leaders involved in committee work with senior administrators and were involved in high-level decision making. As they enter their first professional job search with a master's degree under their belts, these students are somewhat dismayed by the descriptions and responsibilities of the entry-level positions. They often feel overqualified for staff positions that require basic skills.

I began my career as the all-important mail opener in the Harvard Medical School Admissions Office. Yes, I was the one who sent out the acceptance and rejection letters. In the fall semester, I would open the paper applications and alphabetically organize them into piles for the admissions committee, sadly place the rejected applications in a file cabinet, and enter demographic data about the candidates. As exciting as it may sound to place thousands of letters through the letter-folding machine and then seal the envelopes, the job did get somewhat tedious, boring, and humiliating at times. Some of my other jobs included making photocopies of applications and playing caterer. Every week, I would order and set up the food for the admissions committee.

As an undergraduate, I had led admissions tours and information sessions. I talked to parents and potential applicants with enthusiasm, acting as a mini-expert on my beloved college. Ironically, now that I had my bachelor's degree, the only job I could land in higher education was secretary/mail opener. I longed for the days when I was able to talk directly to prospective students and discuss with them their hopes and plans for attending the institution. It was quite embarrassing when friends and family would comment on how impressive it was to be working at such a prestigious institution. But when I revealed my actual duties, I usually was met with a delayed pause followed by a response like, "Oh, at least you're getting some experience."

During my hour-plus commute each day, I would dream of someday actually being able to move beyond paperwork and work directly with students—the precise reason I felt compelled to enter student affairs work. Ten years later, looking back on it, it was far from a wasted year. I learned the inner workings of an admissions office, observed many senior administrators' practices, and laid a practical foundation for the academic course work in my master's degree program the following year.

I truly believe that if you ask any dean or vice president of students, he or she will have a story or two to share about entering the field. Although it might not be stamping envelopes, it certainly wasn't enacting student affairs policies and meeting with boards of trustees.

LESSONS FROM ABROAD

JOHN M. HOWE

In 2007 my routine life as a doctoral student was given a drastic jolt when I opened an e-mail asking if I would be interested in a unique position to create student affairs structures at the American University of Afghanistan in Kabul. I certainly wondered what role student affairs could or should play in this war-torn country, but I found the idea too intriguing to dismiss. I accepted a 2-month position and spent the summer of 2007 at this young university, supported by grant funding from the U.S. Agency for International Development. My main focus was to work with a group of Afghan students to fashion structures for student governance and student organizations. I worked with a dedicated group of students to craft a student constitution and election codes, and hold the first student government elections in the nation in nearly 30 years. The excitement surrounding this event was palpable, and more than 81% of the student body voted in the election. Certainly, my initial concerns about the desire of students to be involved in university life proved to be unfounded.

My 2 months at the American University of Afghanistan passed quickly, and I began to have tinges of regret. While students were certainly excited about voting, would the elected students carry out their responsibilities? While I was cleaning out my office, the newly elected student body vice president stopped in to say goodbye. At the end of our conversation he said that he should ask for two hairs. He proceeded to inform me that according to Afghan tradition, if I was needed in the future, he would burn a hair and I would know to return. I was touched by this conversation and this young man's excitement and anticipation of the year to come.

While I left no hair with this young man, my genetic make-up certainly is predisposed to the loss of many a follicle on any given day. I am not certain if a hair was burned or not, but much to my surprise and my family's dismay, I found myself bound for Kabul the following summer as well. The tasks for my return to Kabul were to teach a university success course for students entering the undergraduate program and to create housing structures for the growing university. I was also eager to contact student government members to learn of their successes and difficulties in their year of service.

I quickly learned the answers to my queries surrounding student government upon my return. Although student government lacked a litany of accomplishments, they had managed to achieve minor programmatic goals and strived to represent the student body of the institution. This was no small feat, as students were quite unfamiliar with formalized student governance structures. While the student government might have seemed like a weak body to a western eye, the elected members sculpted and changed the organizational structures to meet the needs of Afghan learners. It was certainly uplifting to see that student involvement in Kabul was alive and well.

During my year away, the student body grew exponentially, and more and more students from the provinces were in need of housing. I was tasked with overseeing the move from the rented house for provincial young men to a larger home. While hardly recognizable to a western campus filled with residence halls, the men's dormitory could comfortably house 30 Afghan men. To create as positive a living-learning community as possible, a recreation room, complete with pool table, was placed in the basement and a study area on the ground floor. By the middle part of the summer, the new home was nearly complete, and housing assignments for our new dormitory were made. I made great efforts to ensure that rooms were not filled to capacity immediately. Quad rooms were initially triples, and triples were made doubles until the boarding population required the rooms' maximum occupancy. But this western notion of space was lost upon Afghan learners used to sharing accommodations, and they immediately requested additional roommates. This was one of the many examples of my decisions, rooted in western values, conflicting with the needs of Afghan learners.

Living in a war-torn land certainly affects one's perception of time. One often hears "In'shallah" at the end of a phrase, indicating that the future depends on the will of Allah. For instance, when I said, "See you tomorrow" to my group of evening students, "In'shallah" was the common response. On the day of the residence transfer, our procurement officer informed me that the move would take place at 10:30 a.m. At 10:30, I dutifully took a university vehicle to the men's residence and was happy to see piles of belongings bundled together or placed in large plastic zippered bags. However, the vinyl tablecloth with the remains of breakfast still lay on the living room floor. Initially I was upset. "Why is this still here? The truck will arrive at any minute." A few minutes later, a few of the young men came strolling down the stairs, offered me tea, and sat down for breakfast of nan (local flat bread) and jam. Thirty minutes passed. A large metal tray was loaded with the dirty tea glasses and rubbish, and the vinyl tablecloth was folded up and taken to the kitchen. About five of the residents sat on the couches and turned on the television, flicking through stations that seemed to show an extraordinary number of soap operas from around the globe dubbed into Dari. It was odd to see these young men mocking the emotional outbursts of characters from China, India, and Great Britain. They stopped briefly on an episode of *CSI* but settled on a documentary of the making of *Rambo* that was in English with Dari subtitles. It was not until 11:45 a.m. that the truck and hired laborers arrived. The young men seemed unfazed and were content to move to their more spacious home. The residence move happened not on a western schedule, but in Afghan time.

I miss the conversations with the students, particularly the residents of the men's dormitory and students from my class. I appreciated the tenacity of the resident assistant I hired. He fearlessly asked for items for the house on a daily basis, although my answer was rarely affirmative. One day I asked him why he kept asking for things when my answer was almost always no. He smiled and said, "Well, you might say yes." My students seemed to have this same mentality and used each returned paper as the start of a negotiation process and an attempt to bargain for a higher grade. I think the future of Afghan businesses is in safe hands with the students I encountered over these two summers.

These students certainly pestered, entertained, enlightened, taught, and touched my heart in immeasurable ways. The language, cultural, societal, and religious differences between us were great, but hardly insurmountable. Through mutual care, respect, and concern for each other, these chasms of difference were significantly lessened, as if in testament to the Dari proverb that says, "There is a way from heart to heart." The life experiences and struggles that these students have faced in their young lives could certainly make many bitter, but they choose to seek opportunity instead. I left Kabul with the utmost respect for these young people and truly believe that Afghanistan's future is bright if they are able to play any role in the nation's development. As student affairs professionals, that anticipation for a better future is, after all, our hope for all students, regardless of where they reside.

The Day Jesus Christ Visited

James D. Hardwick

I remember the day Jesus Christ visited me at Saint John's University. The landscape of Saint John's University in Collegeville, Minnesota, is dominated by a concrete and glass abbey church fronted by a large concrete bell banner on four legs. The dramatic bell banner with its row of five bells serves as a beacon to the campus, and the ringing bells call the monks of the Benedictine monastic community to prayer. I had been warned by our director of life safety services that the visibility of the bell banner attracts both the faithful and the mentally ill.

As the new dean of campus life, I was working in my office in the university's recently constructed campus center. As I had started the position only 3 weeks earlier, I found myself with frequent visitors from the faculty, staff, and monastic community who wanted to introduce themselves. On the day Jesus Christ visited me, I was not surprised to see an unfamiliar man enter the reception area for our office suite. I went out to the reception area, introduced myself, and asked the man if I could help him.

The man shook my outstretched hand, looked at me intently, and said, "I am Jesus Christ." Without missing a beat, I replied, "It is a pleasure to meet you, Jesus."

Looking over the shoulder of Jesus to the main hallway, I noticed our director of life safety services standing outside our doorway talking on his radio. I learned later that he had been called by a staff member from the bookstore to alert him to the fact that Jesus Christ was in the building. He arrived in time to see me engage Jesus Christ in conversation.

"What brings you to Saint John's University, Jesus?" I asked as nonchalantly as possible. "I am here to meet with the monks in the abbey church," Jesus replied.

"Do the monks know that you are coming?" I asked. I immediately smiled to myself after hearing my own question. Of course the monks would know that Jesus Christ would be coming. Maybe not today, I acknowledged to myself, but the next coming of Jesus was not exactly a secret.

"No," replied Jesus. "I need to talk to the abbot."

I looked at the wall clock in our outer-office reception area and noticed that we had 2 more hours before the bells in the bell banner would ring to call the monks to prayer. I did not want the bells to interrupt our conversation before we could ascertain what plans Jesus Christ had for the monks.

"I notice that it is almost 3 p.m.," I told Jesus. "The monks won't be gathering for prayer for another 2 hours. Would you like me to find an escort to take you to the abbot's office?" I offered. Jesus agreed to have an escort take him to the abbot.

"I could ask a colleague to bring a vehicle to the front of this building to give you a ride." I watched the director of life safety services smile at my offer, nod his head, and notify our security dispatcher to have a patrol officer bring a vehicle for transport of our guest. Again, Jesus agreed to the suggestion.

Knowing that I needed to stall for time until the vehicle was in place, I had an inspiration. I hoped the question would not upset Jesus or risk my own salvation. "Do you see a doctor or a psychiatrist?" I asked Jesus earnestly. "As a matter of fact, I do," Jesus replied. "I see Dr. Paul Anderson."

I glanced over to the hallway to see our director of life safety services smiling and jotting down the name of the health care professional. I hoped the doctor was a mental health care professional.

"Where does Dr. Anderson have his office?" I asked Jesus. "He is located in St. Paul, Minnesota," came the reply.

I asked Jesus what he wanted to discuss with the abbot and the monks. I listened politely as Jesus rambled on about sin, repenting, and the power of prayer. After a few long minutes, I heard the director of life safety services clear his throat as he entered our reception area. I introduced him to Jesus Christ, and told him that Jesus was interested in meeting with the abbot and the monks. I asked him if he had a vehicle available to give Jesus Christ a ride. I shook hands with Jesus and thanked him for his visit, and watched the two men walk out of our office suite and down the hallway to the waiting vehicle.

Later, I learned that Jesus Christ was driven to our local hospital and admitted to the psychiatric ward. His doctor in St. Paul, Minnesota—about 2 hours east of campus—had been notified of the visit of Jesus Christ to our campus.

The irony of the encounter with Jesus Christ was not lost on me. After all, on a stone obelisk in front of the abbey church at Saint John's University is a reminder from the Rule of Benedict: *Treat all guests as if they were Christ.* I wondered if the next coming of Jesus Christ would be handled any differently.

THE LUCKY BLUE STONE

ROBYN HUDSON

There are powerful and magical objects in my life. I have a smooth, royal blue stone. The deep, shining blue is marbled with midnight black flecks and thin ribbons of metallic gold. The size of half a bar of soap, it fits perfectly into the palm or pocket. It's not bulky, but weighs just enough so one feels its presence. A student named Ben gave it to me. He picked it up in Afghanistan at the end of a tour of duty where he experienced gunfights and exploding rockets. I helped Ben with the challenge of earning a 4-year degree between periods of active military service. I humbly accepted his gift.

I assist students with disabilities who struggle with academic performance. My official title is "academic coach," so students will anticipate a collaborative, positive, and action-oriented experience. Academic coaching is usually a two-semester, intensive, voluntary program. Students in academic coaching learn about their specific disabilities, including learning disabilities, attention deficit hyperactivity disorder, brain injuries, and severe medical conditions. They come to understand how a disability affects life and learning.

Through the process of academic coaching, students design and implement strategies, both traditional and creative, to build up strengths and meet goals. Students borrow the lucky blue stone to help them accomplish something that has high stakes. It seems to work when really needed. But it wasn't me who revealed the stone's power. That's where JJ comes in.

JJ was an international doctoral student attempting to pass her qualifying exams in a major I knew little about. She had already failed her qualifying exams twice. Usually, that would result in expulsion from the program and a plane ticket back to her home country, an emerging third-world nation. A PhD was her means to elevate her standard of living and provide security for her family. JJ had a job at a university in her home country that was contingent upon completion of the PhD. Her research would assist people in her home village. She was genuinely talented. JJ's course work was strong and the faculty supported her. No one could figure out why she was failing.

JJ came to me on referral but was doubtful that anyone could help her. JJ possessed natural strength and beauty, but it was shadowed by fear and distress. JJ feared that people perceived how dysfunctional, stupid, and worthless she felt. For cultural reasons, and because her self-esteem was low, JJ was not able to make eye contact. Her young child lived with her while her husband was working in the home country. A family member came to the States to provide child care, but defected and disappeared. JJ was overwhelmed, with very little support. Trapped in a spiral of helplessness and avoidance, she cut off contact with her department.

My assumptions told me it was hopeless. Getting involved with this student was going to take tremendous energy. It did not seem worth it. At the same time, something told me not to write her off just yet. JJ was desperate for something to grasp onto. I offered her some promises I was not sure I could keep. I assured her I would help her, that I would figure something out, and that she could count on me. That seemed to be enough for the day. She left with my business card and an invitation to meet with me regularly. When JJ left, I sat back and closed my eyes and tried to figure out what we were going to do.

JJ was so distraught during our first month of meetings that all she could do was cry and apologize. I was understanding, flexible, and compassionate, but the opportunity for action was fading fast. At first, it was difficult to tailor study strategies for a grueling qualifier. Memorization, repetition, critical analysis, and practice are key elements for tough exams. We worked on mastering these components. She initiated contact with her professors and other students to prepare for the exam.

Things improved for a time. Then suddenly, her husband visited, informed her of an extramarital affair, and took their child back to his country to be raised by relatives. It was devastating, a major setback, but there was no way she was giving up. JJ refocused on the work because it was the only chance she had of attaining the resources and power to see her child again. Her home empty, I invited JJ to study all day in a vacant office next to mine. Five months passed too quickly for JJ, and the day of the qualifiers arrived.

Just before the exam, JJ came in for a pep talk. I picked up the lucky stone and told her about Ben. As I hoped she would, JJ asked if she could keep it until she got the results. She placed it in her pocket. The outcome of the qualifier would be posted within a week. Seven days passed with no news. Three more days and another weekend went by, and still no JJ. The waiting was torture, but I would not allow myself to think that she had failed. Two weeks after the exam, she appeared at my office door and held out the stone. "It *is* lucky," she said, "I passed." We jumped up and down, hugged, and cried.

That was not the end of her academic journey. There was a proposal, dissertation, and defense. There were more tears and more cheers. For her dissertation defense, she borrowed the stone again. She returned it several days later to tell me how well things went. JJ was exhausted and ecstatic, but mostly she was ready to go home. Her flight was leaving in a few days, so we wished each other the best. That was the last time I saw her.

The blue stone comes and goes from its shelf. Students borrow it for luck. Yet, the more it works, the less I rely on luck. The magic comes from seeing others win their battles, despite the odds of disability, circumstance, and past losses. Still, many falter and fail, no matter how much effort they exert. Even with years of being a coach and counselor, I am utterly unable to predict who will make it. The ones who do leave legacies remind me to avoid assumptions and keep fighting. When I get frustrated and assume the worst, I hold the blue stone and think about Ben, JJ, and many others. I thank them and wish them luck.

AM I WRONG TO BELIEVE A SERVICE CLUB SHOULD ACT MATURE?

LYNETTE S. MERRIMAN

I was a freshman. Even though our door was wide open, my roommate Jamie and I were trying to study. The yelling and screaming from our hall mates was getting louder and louder. I got up to close the door, but before I could reach it, a male student came charging into our room, knocking everything in his path onto the ground, and emptying the contents of our cabinets and drawers all over our floor. In the midst of his ransacking, he incessantly screamed something unintelligible and then he fled—as quickly as he appeared. I was mad, really mad. Jamie and I both had a midterm the next day.

I cautiously walked out into the hall, where I was greeted by floor mates who were equally upset by this plundering act. I was soon told that we had been victims of an initiation into one of the university's male service organizations. Yes, "service" organization, one that represented the university during special events. Instead of studying, I wanted to complain—but to whom? As a naïve freshman, I did not know where to go. As a journalism student, I ultimately decided to voice my complaint by submitting a letter to the editor of our student newspaper. I typed up my grievance that evening, marched over to the student union, went to the fourth floor, and dropped the grievance off in the newspaper office. Since the office was a flurry of activity—no doubt trying to meet deadlines—I thought nothing would come of my journalistic effort, but at least I felt better having vented.

Two days later a classmate came up to me and said, "Great letter."

My complaint was actually published—verbatim! All these years later, I don't remember much of the text, but I do remember my closing sentence: "Am I wrong to believe a service club should act mature?" This was great! My voice was heard.

Later that week I received a call. The dean of students wanted to meet with me. I was not informed of the reason for the meeting and, quite honestly, I had no idea what a "dean of students" was or did. I was nervous: "Dean" was in his title. I apprehensively made the appointment.

As I entered the vice president's suite I was quite nervous, thinking I must have done something horribly wrong. As soon as I saw him—a white-haired man wearing a professorial tweed jacket and a warm, gentle, genuine smile—I realized I had nothing to fear.

"Lynette, I want to thank you for writing your letter to the student paper," he said. "I am so sorry you and other students had to go through that." This gentle—and I do mean gentle—man went on to say that such debauchery is not to be tolerated and that the president of the organization would soon be apologizing to me in person. Wow! I liked this dean of students guy!

We talked a little more and he asked about my freshman year and my home town. We soon discovered we were both midwesterners, born in Duluth. This California school no longer seemed so foreign. Over the rest of my undergraduate career, I would periodically see the dean on campus. Each time I was struck by how warm and welcoming he was to me and all students.

Years passed and I settled into a career in higher education—mostly in academic units—recruiting, admitting, and advising students along with other student affairs work. In 2001, I was hired as a student troubleshooter/case manager in the very same vice president's office where I had had my meeting with the dean so many years ago. When I started the job, I thought of him. I thought about how kind he was and how, because of him, a student organization was held accountable, and a freshman was made to feel that she mattered. I thought about how I could make students feel that they mattered.

Today, I understand student affairs from the inside. To those outside the profession, I often describe it as part teacher, part counselor, and part advocate. I believe that these three elements are the foundation of our work. When I met with the dean that day, he clearly exhibited these three qualities. He also made it clear to me that student affairs work involves the heart. Heart is exactly what came through in my meeting with the dean, and it is what I try to exhibit in my work with students every day. Each day as I teach, counsel, and advocate, I hope I do so in the dean's warm and welcoming way. Each day I also read the letters to the editor. I have yet to see a complaint about a ransacking, immature service organization, but if I do, I know how I will respond.

When All the Doors Seem Closed, Find a Window

April Heiselt

My "job-job," as I like to call it, is faculty member who teaches in a student affairs program. My other "job" is to help coordinate the service learning on our campus. Thus, I sit on the fence between practitioner and faculty. This can sometimes be an uncomfortable position, as I don't always fit perfectly into either world. For example, sometimes I try to convince my student affairs colleagues to do research with me. Some of my faculty colleagues tell me that they can't understand why I give so much service to my students. Despite my place on the fence, I love it. I have an opportunity to "play" in both worlds, and to me it is a beautiful marriage!

After working at my institution for a few years, I started to notice that something was lacking on our campus. What was needed fit into the student affairs realm, but I wasn't sure how to make it happen.

I started doing some research and then went to a student affairs colleague I thought could open some doors and shed some light on my idea. He thought it was a great idea, too, but he said, "You'll never make it happen. There won't be anyone who will support you."

With my bubble burst and my emotions deflated, I went back to my office. Dejected, I tried to move on and not think about my idea. That made it worse. I started to think about all the people who had great ideas and didn't give up. What about Thomas Edison, Alexander Graham Bell, the Wright Brothers? They never gave up.

While my idea wasn't quite on par with the Wright Brothers, I knew it had the "right stuff" and that I could make this happen if I tried hard enough. My great idea was to create a community service day to bring faculty, staff, and students together to serve. Sounds great, right? But, I had no money, no committee, and no one to help. I did what we do best in student affairs: I started to talk, to make connections, and to network.

During some of my initial conversations, I was told that a community service day had never been done on our campus and that it was destined to fail. Several colleagues told me that I should be content with my service learning work. I had some dejected days and thought I would give up the idea.

Not knowing what to do next, I thought about academic affairs. I decided to give them a go. It couldn't hurt. I made an appointment with the provost. Our provost is a wonderful, intelligent man. Despite this, he intimidated me. Although I shouldn't have been nervous, I had nightmares about our meeting. I pictured him at the end of a long, dark hallway. As I walked through the darkness, he seemed to get farther and farther away. When I finally reached him and made my request, he looked at me and laughed in my face. Ouch!

On the day of our meeting, I secretly hoped that the provost would cancel. I thought maybe some big thing would come up. Not something bad, just something that would prevent him from being at our meeting. Unfortunately for me, he didn't cancel. In fact, he sent an e-mail telling me he was looking forward to our meeting. I watched the clock like I was waiting for high noon. When the time came, I went to his office.

His office wasn't at all the way it appeared in my nightmares. It wasn't dark or scary. When we met, he shook my hand, offered me some water, and invited me to sit down. We chatted for a bit, and then we got down to business. I explained that I wanted to have a community service day, to target everyone on campus. I am not sure how long I talked, but as I got to the end, I took a deep breath and went for the big ask. I said, "Do you think you can provide any funding for this event?" My heart was in my throat. He suddenly got a serious look on his face and very slowly he asked, "Well, how much are you talking about?" Out of nowhere I said, "Fifteen hundred dollars?" He said, "I can do that." My heart started beating again and I felt like I could hear a choir singing, "Hallelujah!"

So there I was with $1,500 and nothing else. It felt great and lonely. I started looking around for other opportunities. I looked for a window in those same rooms where the doors previously were shut. I reached out. I found some amazing people who liked the service idea. They agreed to come on board and form a committee. I felt as though I had really accomplished something—and we hadn't even done anything yet! My new-found committee came up with a title for the event, a logo, and an event date, but all we had was $1,500, and that would cover only basic costs. How were we going to fund the rest of this event?

I started to think about what I could do to fix the situation. I needed to fundraise. Getting money from the provost inspired me to ask other unlikely sources for donations. I went to the meat lab on campus and asked if they would donate some pulled pork for lunch for the volunteers. They said yes. I asked dining services if they could donate food, and they said yes. After that, the donations started coming. We were getting closer and closer to our goal, but our biggest hurdle was yet to come.

SLAM! Another door shut. The transportation department couldn't cut us a deal. Transportation was the biggest part of our budget. Although we received some donations, we did not have enough money to transport the students to their community partner sites. All the other donations meant nothing if we couldn't get the students off campus to give service.

Concerned about our dilemma, I looked again for the open window. Although one of my student affairs colleagues didn't support the idea, that didn't mean everyone didn't support it. I visited with the associate vice president of student affairs. I explained my situation and told her how close we were to pulling off the event. She was thrilled and said she would see what she could do. I was hopeful.

At that point, we had nothing else to do but wait. We prepared our first-aid kits, spoke with community partners, ordered T-shirts, and waited. We created our website, sent out fliers with the department of housing's mailings, and waited. I met with the university president and with university relations. We sent e-mails to faculty and staff members to recruit volunteer coordinators for the event. We worked each summer orientation session and passed out hundreds of fliers to students—and we waited.

At each team meeting, I was asked about what was happening financially. I had nothing to tell them. The pressure grew more intense as the event came closer. Then one day, I received an e-mail. The associate vice president of student affairs agreed to give us enough money to cover transportation for the event. We couldn't believe it. We were on!

The day before the event, all the weather forecasters predicted a 90% chance of rain. One of the team members called my house at 11 p.m. to tell me the bad news. I felt physically ill. I couldn't sleep. I had convinced all these people to come help, give money, drive vans, give up time at work, and all for what? A rained-out event? I went to bed, not knowing what the morning would bring. It truly is always darkest before the dawn.

When I woke up, it was dark, so I couldn't tell if it was going to rain. Would the students come? Could we still serve the community partners? What about all the hard work? What would I do with all that meat?

I headed to the event site and saw the members of my team with their bright and smiling faces. We looked up at the sky, and although it was dark grey, it wasn't raining. Despite the dark clouds, staff and faculty volunteers showed up on time and ready to serve. Then the students showed up. Not only did they show up, they brought their friends. We had so many students we had to turn some away!

After the students were transported to their sites, I jumped into a university police vehicle and was escorted to the community service sites. I chatted with students, staff, faculty, and community partners. Everyone was happy. The event was a great success!

When I returned to campus, the students were eating lunch. I watched as they laughed and talked about their day. I saw them exchange cell phone numbers and make promises to get in touch with one another. I noticed that staff and faculty volunteers were saying the same things. This event brought people together. It was amazing to watch.

Following the lunch, a staff member stopped me. She told me that she had worked at the university for more than 10 years and never participated in an event until now. She was glad that the community service day finally came to our university. She made me promise to call her when we were planning our next community service event. I was moved and inspired.

It turned out that our event made local and regional news. We were on television, radio, and in countless newspaper articles. This happened because when the doors were shut, we didn't give up. We looked for the open windows. Sometimes the windows were hard to see, but they were there. The trick was finding them and giving them a shove to get them open.

So whether you are practitioner or faculty, staff or student, risk, try, and keep looking for windows when the doors get closed. Things will always work out—perhaps just not always the way you planned.

The Big Speech

Jacqueline Cooper

I remember reading somewhere that people fear public speaking more than anything else, including snakes and spiders. I can't recall exactly where I read the information. I just tucked the tidbit away in my mental folder labeled "random stuff."

Got a new job! Another move up my career ladder! I became the coordinator for new student orientation at a large public university in the South. During my new employee training, I learned that 600 was the average participant count for the freshmen sessions. I also learned that I had to host the general session and give a speech to this large group. At that very moment, a little mental conspiracy took place. My mind let my "random stuff" folder release a long-buried nugget of information. The long-forgotten thought surfaced: the fear of public speaking…number one thing to fear…fear…public speaking…fear. Ugh!

My training continued. General session was the kick-off experience for orientation participants. Freshmen and their parents were hungry for information that would get them through the 2-day session. From a comfortable perch in the corner of the spacious ballroom, I watched the interim coordinator for new student orientation deliver the big speech during the first general session. I watched him stand behind the podium. Using notes, I heard him deliver enrollment stats and a lot of orientation logistics. I watched the audience sit and robotically stare at him. Even through my fear, I knew the disengagement of the audience was not a good thing. It also occurred to me that after my training ended and I took to the stage, the audience could possibly stare like robots at me, too.

I kept my "random stuff" folder at bay while I seriously thought about what I needed to do. I felt as though the success of the big speech hinged on two things: (1) what I needed to say, and (2) how I said it. I asked myself, "What could I possibly do to diminish the robot stare?"

"Eureka!" I thought, "I will open with a joke! Humor is good." I patted myself on the back. I realized that this was not the most original opening, but I had experienced opening jokes done well countless times. "How difficult could it be?" I remember laughing with those speakers. I decided to get this large and challenging audience to laugh. I also decided to edit my trainer's notes, especially the admission stats. I didn't think the audience really needed to know what percentage of their incoming class finished in the top half of the class.

Six hundred pairs of eyes stared up at me. I had concentrated so hard on what I wanted to say, that I totally forgot about the podium. Should I stand behind it? Like countless scared speakers throughout time, I took to the stage and stood behind the podium. I gripped both sides and held on for dear life. It was a white-knuckle experience.

During the staredown with the audience, I forgot my opening joke! I did a quick mental search. "No, not there. It's gone." I stood there spellbound by yet another form of mental conspiracy: forgetting information. In the quick moments that it took me to digest this horrible fact, I discovered my voice. In finding my voice, I also realized that I was extremely nervous. I was not silenced by the fear of public speaking. I was just nervous. What a relief! I realized deep inside that I could deliver the speech, but I still did not have my opening joke.

Something popped into my mind and I spoke. I went with the truth. I boldly announced that unlike other speakers, I did not have a joke and everyone should be happy because if I had one it would probably sound awful anyway. A murmur of chuckles moved through the audience. That sound was music to my ears. My not having a joke turned out to be a joke. Not bad at all. I exhaled, relaxed a little, and launched into the rest of the big speech.

In closing, I decided to tell participants, "As a courtesy to others, please turn off your cell phones and pagers during breakout sessions." However, that reminder reached the audience with a slight twist. Much to my chagrin, I actually said, "As a courtesy to others, please turn off your cell phones and vibrators during breakout sessions." A silence engulfed the room. Immediately realizing my faux pas, I dropped my head and chuckled. My mind raced. I couldn't believe that I just told a room full of people to turn off their vibrators! Not good. My bosses would definitely hear about this! Even worse, my orientation team would never let me live this down. My smile in place, I slowly looked up and followed with, "Well, I guess I do have a real joke after all." The room roared with laughter.

LEARNING THE HARD WAY

RAYNA A. ISAKI

I learned my lesson the hard way. I am ashamed that I did not take what I learned in class seriously and apply it to my life. I was a naïve freshman when I stepped into a women's studies class, not knowing what feminism was. I attended every class, completed all the readings, and took notes on the professor's lectures, but the material never really sank in. I heard the arguments for feminism, but I was not listening, because I did not care. Although I was uninterested in the topic at the time, the experience that I endured later that semester would completely change my perspective about feminism and leave me deeply engaged in the field.

As a young college female growing up in a century of revolution in women's rights and opportunities, it would make sense that I support the fight for equality, but unfortunately I did not. I was not interested in feminism because I accepted the subordinate status of women and never challenged it. I reasoned that male dominance was ingrained in society and I was convinced there was nothing I could do to change this. I acknowledged what I perceived to be marginal issues facing women—such as the pay gap, familial obligations, and submissiveness to men—but I was too ignorant to see how these smaller issues accumulated into bigger, more serious problems. It was only after I personally experienced the epitome of female oppression that I realized changes in small issues can profoundly affect the larger scheme of things.

When I met my first boyfriend in college, I was attracted to him because of his masculine personality and dominant attitude. From the start, he exhibited power in the relationship by doing small things such as commenting on how I should dress and act. He made all the decisions in our relationship and had strong opinions on what he wanted me to do and not do. In retrospect, I realize that his behavior was controlling, but at that time I found it attractive. I felt protected and comforted by a man who knew exactly want he wanted.

Further into our relationship, he became more dominating and controlling. He put limitations on what I was allowed to do, including restricting my participation in campus organizations, community service, and athletic activities. He also demanded that I stop spending time with my friends. His reason for these restrictions was that these activities were distractions that took me away from my studies. He explained that it was important for me to listen to him because he cared so much about what was best for me.

I attempted several times to argue with my boyfriend about the decisions he forced on me, but he always rejected my pleas. He ended up scolding me for challenging him. By yelling, punching my car, and breaking my cell phone, he threatened me into obeying him. At this point he never physically harmed me, but I was nevertheless scared to stand up for myself, challenge him, or leave the relationship. I desperately longed for his approval, so I did everything he wanted, and by doing so I reinforced my view of women as passive and dutiful. This led me to lose all self-confidence and doubt my competence in making decisions about what was best for me. Although at times I felt he was being irrational and unfair, I always reassured myself that he was just doing what was best for me.

Things worsened one night during an argument when his controlling behavior escalated into violence. I was helpless as he physically overpowered me, and there was nothing I could do except let him act out his rage. When he eventually stopped, I was thankful for my life, but I simultaneously realized that this was enough and something needed to change. After reflecting on what was happening to me in this relationship, I finally made an overwhelming connection: Everything I had learned in my women's studies class was directly applicable to my situation! All the marginal things that oppress women may seem insignificant when viewed individually, but together they accumulate into bigger issues. Relating to my relationship, all the little controlling behaviors my boyfriend exhibited built up to the night he became physical. When I had no problem with him being dominating in our relationship, I sent him the message that he had complete power over me.

The next day I entered my women's studies class with newfound confidence. I realized that I possessed the power to make a difference, a desire to learn what I could do to change things, and an entirely new perspective about women's rights and equality. Although I was initially ashamed to tell my professor about my situation, I sought help from her after class. To my surprise, she was extremely compassionate, understanding, and offered help. She comforted and reassured me that I was not weak for allowing the situation to escalate, but courageous enough to recognize the circumstances and seek help. She referred me to the women's center on campus, which helped me properly terminate my abusive relationship, educated me about these types of situations, and provided assistance for coping with the circumstances.

Although I am only one person against a problem plaguing an entire society, I recognized that I can make a difference. By defending myself I am taking a stand, representing other abused women, and not perpetuating the problem. I learned two important lessons the hard way from this experience. First, I realized the importance of challenging the seemingly marginal issues that oppress women—such as the traditional stereotype of women being submissive—because if it is not confronted, oppression accumulates into bigger issues. If I had defended myself and fought for control in my life at the beginning, maybe the relationship would not have ended in violence. Second, I learned to apply the material learned in class to real-life experiences, because something that may seem uninteresting at the time may be of great use in the future. Today, I am absolutely committed to women's rights issues, and I feel empowered to make other women realize the strength they possess to lead their own lives.

You Look Tired

Carol A. Lundberg

"You look tired," commented a student in my class the other night. I assured her that I was fine. At the 10 p.m. conclusion of that class, a different student asked me if I'd been on campus since my meeting with her that morning. I nodded and said that a long day was okay for me. She told me that I looked tired and that I had looked tired last week as well. My thought: "Yikes—I'm so rundown that they remember it from the previous week!" The next day, my mother called to see if I was okay (I had looked tired over the weekend). I was beginning to get the message. Of course I was tired! On top of my regular workload, I was trying to finish things so I could head out to the American College Personnel Association conference. I'm sure you can relate to this dilemma. Every spring, I think to myself, "Does the benefit of the conference outweigh the effort expended in getting there?" However, by the time I've gained new perspectives from the sessions, felt the embrace of old friends, and enjoyed some informal time with my graduate students, I am always convinced that it is well worth the effort. This year was no different, although a string of events on one particular morning was especially noteworthy.

It all began as I stood in line to purchase a bagel in the mall adjoining my hotel. Ahead of me was a well-dressed woman on her way to work. She yelled into her cell phone that she would no longer call the listener (her ex-husband, I presumed) to tell him to wake the children on the mornings they were with him. Trembling and swearing, she was at the end of her rope. She stated clearly that although she regularly called him every morning to be sure he woke up the children, she would no longer call. She explained why he should be able to do this on his own, why it was not her responsibility to call, and why she would stop doing it. In print, this sounds like a strong and healthy response, but the woman was terrified. She was worried, afraid that the children she loved so dearly would not make it to school on time, that they might get less than they deserved simply because she was unwilling to enable their father to be irresponsible. She dug in her purse for the correct change to pay for her bagel, although the phone conversation distracted her from effectively accomplishing this feat. The bagel seller, aware of the drama on the phone, responded with, "It's okay—I'll get it from you tomorrow." It was a moment of grace. Witnessing that moment took away some of my tiredness.

My next stop was a session in which several prominent women in the field described how they structured their careers in ways that embraced multiple priorities and values, each with a different configuration. Having already traversed many of the crossroads that would be discussed in the session, I was eager to hear the dialogue and to feel the energy in the room. The questions and worries of younger women were as inspiring to me as the comments from the more experienced panelists. However, the remark that moved me the most came from Susan Komives when she offhandedly commented about a year in her life that was so full of family and work responsibilities that all her houseplants died. It was clear that letting the plants die was a no-brainer to her. Better than the comment was the air with which she said it. She chuckled. Plants are minor. This, again, was a moment of grace. There are some things in my life that are less important than others. If Susan Komives can let her plants die, then it's no crime that my kitchen will never make it into *Real Simple* or that my pedicure wore out 6 months ago.

When it was time for the closing session with Carol Gilligan, I began to feel the pull back to reality, which, for me, was filled with papers to grade. I was tempted to pick up my red pen and skip the session. Fortunately, I let my better judgment win and found a seat in a ballroom bursting with luggage and student affairs professionals who were beginning to think about the things awaiting them on their return. Those thoughts would be interrupted by 60 minutes with Carol Gilligan. I heard the narrative of her life and how it intersected with, informed, and enlightened her theory about multiple voices that are lost. I was reminded of the women in the earlier session who wondered if they could be both PTA president and associate dean. I thought of the women who asked questions that were not safe to ask at their particular institutions, questions about the route to the presidency, about coming out to students, about the intersection of the personal and professional aspects of their lives. There is energy in those voices, perspective in those voices, and I don't hear them enough in my nonconference life. Perhaps, I just don't listen.

Gilligan argued in her talk, as in her book, that the "different voice" is not necessarily a female voice, but a voice that can be held by men or women. I wondered about the different voices that are silenced in my classroom, in my office, in my living room. What am I missing when it's not okay to say something? I was thankful for the woman yelling at her ex-husband on the cell phone in the bakery line. Her voice gave me perspective. I was thankful that Susan Komives told us about her dead philodendrons. It gave me hope. I was thankful that my students felt comfortable telling me that I looked tired. It gave me a dose of reality. I traveled to Atlanta with a list of things I needed to accomplish. That list was long, detailed, timelined, and precise. Everything on it was about my work. I traveled home with that list intact, but I had another list as well. Some things on the second list were switch from white rice to brown rice, visit Mom, and spend more time in the produce aisle.

There is a voice that is missing from academia, a voice that recognizes that we are whole people. In student affairs, we often discuss how we might bridge the gap between student affairs and academic affairs or between the curricular and cocurricular, but there is another chasm we seldom discuss. That divide is between the personal and professional, between who I am and what I bring to work. When that divide is too wide, I get worn out. When my students and colleagues don't see me beaming over my daughter's photo award, they see only a part of me. In *The Courage to Teach,* Parker Palmer comments about the absurdity of our requirement that students always write in the third person, forcing them to delete their own voice.[2] In my rush to be productive and professional, I often overlook the need, both for my students and myself, to bring our stories, our histories, and our whole selves to the classroom. Perhaps this is why I get tired.

---

2   Palmer, P. (1997). *The courage to teach: Exploring the inner landscape of a teacher's life.* San Francisco: Jossey-Bass.

DEREK'S BURDEN

LINDA M. LEMIESZ

Although electromagnetics is often the bane of engineering students, the physics instructor had never seen a case like this in 20 years of teaching. Derek, he reported, faithfully attended all classes, and received As on every surprise quiz. Despite the apparently successful preparation, Derek had failed to show up for the first midterm. When the professor asked for an explanation, Derek offered none. That morning, Derek had missed the second midterm. His cumulative grade in the class was a D.

"Linda," the professor said, "I've failed a fair number of students in my physics class over the years, but I've never previously failed someone who understood the material. There must be some explanation. Please see if you can get him to talk to you."

The student was a commuter. Checking with his advisor and his other professors, I found no explanation for his inability to appear for physics exams. I wondered if this could possibly be some sort of panic disorder, although his performance on pop quizzes seemed to rule out this possibility. I called Derek and asked him to make an appointment.

Several weeks passed before he presented himself. Superficially, nothing seemed to be the matter. He showed no sign of depression or substance abuse and appeared to be a robust 18-year-old male. I knew he had attended a stellar local high school famed for its science and engineering graduates, so my first questions attempted to determine whether he was still interested in pursuing a career in electrical engineering. Maybe he needed to flunk out of school to convince his parents that engineering was not right for him?

Derek's answers were brief, but he was enthusiastic about engineering and physics. His responses shed no light on why he missed the two examinations. I decided to confront the issue.

"Derek, the professor would be willing to give you a make-up examination for the second exam if you have some sort of medical excuse. He feels you understand the material, and he does not want to put you in a position where you have to repeat the class. This might be more important than you realize, because it will take you out of the sequence of courses you need to complete before you begin your electrical engineering electives next year. You don't want to fall a year behind. Is something going on medically that we can get a doctor to excuse?"

Derek looked startled by this piece of information. Softly, he said, "I really do not have a medical excuse." For the first time in our conversation, I sensed that there was something else he might be willing to divulge if I could only figure out the correct question to ask. I reiterated, "The professor is trying to help you. Rather than ask you a direct question and risk embarrassing you, he has asked me to intervene. Is there some problem impacting your attendance? Where were you during those exams?"

With some hesitation, Derek admitted that he was in a hospital emergency room during both examinations.

"Then you should be able to get your doctor to write a note attesting to that fact, so that the professor will give you a make-up examination," I said.

Derek said immediately, "But the doctor didn't know I was there."

Light began to dawn. "You were there on behalf of someone else, weren't you?" Occasionally, a student has to intervene in his roommate or friend's medical emergency, enduring the interminable delay in a city emergency room. Often, such episodes involve substance abuse and thus embarrassment for all parties. Still, most students would not risk missing exams twice.

But the story Derek blurted out had a plotline I had never heard before. His roommate was not an 18-year-old co-adventurer, but his 76-year-old father. The death of his mother had left him the custodian of his surviving parent. His older sisters, overwhelmed with the needs of their own children, had no time to help him. Derek alone managed the daily care of his elderly and infirm parent. When his father fell, Derek took him to the emergency room.

Our college had systems in place to identify students who had dependent siblings or children, but nothing to indicate which students were caring for their parents. It occurred to me that Derek's situation could be a harbinger of things to come. How many of the babies born to middle-aged parents would, as teenagers, have the burden of geriatric care thrust onto them? How as a college could we help them?

We worked out a system in which Derek could be excused from classes and exams as needed. He submitted documentation from his father's physician about his father's ongoing frailness. Under this system, Derek thrived. He remained a strong student and managed to participate in a variety of school clubs. We were deeply impressed by Derek's stoicism, his grace about handling family care issues, his apparent lack of resentment about not having the social life of the average college student. His dad, we agreed, must be very proud to have such an exceptional man for his son.

At graduation, we could see Derek's sisters in the audience with an elderly man, clearly Derek's father. At the end of the ceremony, we rushed over to congratulate the family. "You must be so proud of your son, the electrical engineer," I said. I was met with a vacant look. It seemed that Derek had concealed one other family secret. His now-80-year-old parent and roommate had advanced Alzheimer's disease. The man was no longer capable of realizing that his devoted caretaker was his youngest child, a son who had just earned his diploma in one of the most challenging academic fields. Wordlessly, I watched as Derek tenderly lifted his father from his chair, placed him in a wheelchair, and pushed him up the aisle. Throughout that slow voyage, Derek's mortarboard never slipped.

The Annals of Improbable Judicial Affairs

Matthew Birnbaum

I dedicate this story to judicial affairs professionals who frequently have to deal with the improbable and unlikely.

A few years ago, I sat on a panel adjudicating a case involving an altercation between two male students. The panel of three administrators first spoke to Rick, a first-year student, who claimed that another student called him a "f..king Mexican" and told him to go home. As a second-generation Mexican American, Rick stated that he had experienced racism before and, after much reflection, he decided to confront the person.

Three administrators, myself included, were proud of Rick's conviction and were equally outraged by the conduct of the other student. We asked Rick to leave the room and mutually agreed that racist behavior must have severe consequences.

We then called in Mike, the other student involved in the altercation. Mike, a Caucasian, claimed that Rick had simply walked up to him shouting, "What did you say?" and tried to start a fight.

We believed each student's impassioned version of the incident but could not figure out how both could be accurate. We called both students into the room and had them explain in detail their version of events in front of each other. Here is what we learned:

Both students were walking in opposite directions through a dimly lit parking lot in the middle of the night, and both were talking to their girlfriends on their cell phones. As they passed each other, Mike said to his girlfriend, "Unbelievable! Do they even know you're a f..king Mexican? You should really just go home." Mike was upset when he learned that his friends had made some racially offensive jokes in front of his girlfriend, who was born and raised in Mexico.

The moment after Mike made his comment, Rick's cell phone connection dropped. Speaking loudly into the phone he asked, "What did you say? Speak up, I didn't hear what you said." Rick stopped walking and snapped his cell phone shut.

Mike, believing that he was speaking too loudly, turned and told Rick, "Sorry, I didn't know you could hear me." As they faced each other, Rick processed some of the words he heard Mike say: "f..king Mexican...go home." He said to Mike, "What did you say?"

Mike began to feel threatened. "Dude, it's none of your business. I wasn't talking to you," Mike responded. This exchange occurred a few more times, leaving each student feeling more confused and threatened in the dark parking lot. With each exchange, they inched toward the other, raising their voices, and thus escalating the situation. Within seconds, they were pushing each other harder and harder with each verbal exchange. Fortunately, campus security happened to pass by before anyone was hurt.

Improbable as it sounds, as best as we could tell, this is what happened. Finding an appropriate sanction for the students was not going to be easy. We dismissed the students and stared at each other, not knowing what to think. The first words came from a fellow administrator whom I had never heard tell a joke. "Unbelievable," she said, "and I thought talking on the phone while driving was dangerous."

From a Person to a Profile

Scott C. Brown

O n a recent flight out to California, I boarded a plane with my wife and three small children. My wife and my then-4-year-old daughter were in the aisle and middle seats. Next to them was a 30-something man with a dark complexion. I thought he was of Middle Eastern origin. He wore a T-shirt, shorts, sandals with tube socks, a baseball cap, and a 3-day-old beard. He had a ready smile. When I looked over, he was making my daughter laugh while engaging my wife in easy conversation. Shortly after takeoff, my two older kids and I watched the in-flight movie. The others took naps.

After the film ended and we were about an hour from arriving in Los Angeles, my wife looked distractedly at the empty seat beside her and asked, "Where did he go?" I said, "He's probably in the bathroom." She remarked, "He's been gone a long time," and went back to reading. I looked down the aisle and did not see him standing outside the lavatory or anywhere else. I didn't go back to reading.

I needed to find out where he was. A small bead of distrust wormed its way into the base of my skull. In a millisecond, thoughts of a shoe bomber or some other 9/11 nightmare flickered in my mind. Didn't he fit some sort of profile? I strode down the aisle with increasing purpose, my anxiety growing. Then, when I got near the back of the plane, I stopped abruptly. There he was, sitting quietly in the back seat reading *People* magazine. He just wanted some peace and quiet. I realized what I had just done. As quickly as my fear of this man had grown, it dissipated, replaced by shame.

I needed to assuage my guilt, so I struck up a conversation with him.

I learned that he was born in Pakistan, had lived in Southern California for many years, and now lives in Florida. He owns a Mexican restaurant and speaks fluent Spanish. Each fact I learned about him revealed a gracious and ordinary man. I was a friendly stranger just chatting him up, despite my shameful pretext. His crime of "flying while Arab" was in progress. Here I was willing and ready to make a citizen's arrest. The true scene of this crime was not the interior of the plane, but the interior of my soul. My bias was sharp and unvarnished. It was over in a moment, but the scar is ugly, hidden, and deep.

Now that I am safely on the ground, the earth beneath my feet feels uncertain. I am trying to understand how this flash of fear reared up. On one hand, human beings are capable of infinite acts of kindness. We can find many extraordinary examples of heroism by ordinary individuals, even in times of personal peril, fear, and sacrifice. On the other hand, cruelty is also an innately human trait, well within the spectrum of our capabilities. In a debased roll call of the last half century, we can find many large-scale examples of our lowest selves: the Holocaust, Bosnia, Rwanda, Sudan, and even the internment of American citizens.

Yes, humans are capable of terrible things. But shouldn't I be able to stem that unsavory impulse? My personal convictions have led me to help others as the primary focus of my higher education work—not just my living, but also my life. As a student affairs professional and as a person, I have always made conscious decisions to equip myself to better do so. I strive to understand and tame my biases and assumptions. I am a professional in a field that is at the forefront of these issues of tolerance and acceptance, a field that buoys my best self to be an incessant agent of good. Ironically, I had just invited our Muslim chaplain into our staff meeting to talk about any particular needs of Muslim students, especially during Ramadan. As a seasoned student affairs professional, shouldn't I be "finished business"? I teach and train others on this stuff. I often get a free pass in many circumstances because we are "preaching to the choir." But the choir always needs practice.

The animal behaviorist Konrad Lorenz argues that that there are many examples of aggression everywhere in nature, and the most dangerous moment is the combustible intersection of fear and anger. A mother defending her young or an animal backed in a corner. As human beings, we are always able to somehow find ourselves a corner. I have always

109

avoided unnecessary conflict and have never been in a fistfight, even as a child. But what would I do to protect my life? My family?

I was 30,000 feet in the air, but I'd never felt so low. I was vain enough to believe that because of my rational efforts, I was inoculated against this type of irrational reaction. Some would argue that this is a reasonable response to an unreasonable time. Perhaps. I never kid myself about what allows people to do bad things. I never underestimate evil's power. I just underestimated it in me. I am a student affairs professional. But in the right, terrible circumstance, perhaps I am capable of anything. In the words of Paul "Bono" Hewson, "I can't change the world, but I can change the world in me." It is a pretty big place.

Highest Degree of Importance

Linda Gillingham

E very now and then, a phone call will come into the office of under-graduate academic services that begins something like this: "I was a student back in 19__." Usually, if the call is transferred to me, it means that the student did not actually graduate. The odds are also pretty good that the caller thinks that he or she *did* graduate.

Thus began the call from Paul on a late Friday afternoon in early August 2007. It was Paul's last day at his current job. He had accepted a new position, which was to begin the following Monday. His future employer called our registrar's office to verify Paul's undergraduate de-gree, only to receive the response, "We cannot verify that degree." This is what elicited Paul's call.

I explained to Paul that he did not graduate in August 1998. His re-sponse was disbelief, followed by another not-so-rare comment in similar situations: "But I walked in the ceremony and everything!" The longer we talked, the more distraught he became. I'll never forget the despera-tion in his voice as he said, "You've got to be kidding. I'll lose my job and my wife and my house!"

We continued to talk beyond office closing time. I explained the reasons why he had not graduated. He shared with me an astounding fact: After he left our institution, he went on to complete a master's de-gree and begin a doctoral program! I had visions of a frazzled admissions counselor on his or her first day on the job, accidentally forgetting to check Paul's transcript for "degree awarded."

Finally, Paul ended the conversation by thanking me for talking with him so late on a Friday. He said he would talk with his wife over the weekend, try to regroup, and then call me again on Monday.

Subsequent to this initial call, Paul and I talked often. We discussed transfer credit options, possibilities for seeking removals of incompletes, ideas for contacting professors regarding independent study options, possibilities for online classes, and other conceivable long shots. Bottom line was that Paul accepted his new position but was given just one semester to complete his undergraduate degree. This meant completing 16 credits in less than 4 months, while working full time in a new job.

Paul and I later laughed as we looked back on our seemingly regular schedule of Friday afternoon phone conversations, during which we worked out each detail. Basically, with a combination of all of the above options, Paul was able to complete all requirements for his degree on December 14, 2007, which was his employer's exact deadline. On Friday, December 14, I faxed a letter to his employer in Florida, verifying that Paul's degree was awarded.

During my final Friday afternoon phone conversation with Paul, he was so elated that he could hardly contain himself. He even put his wife on the phone, who was equally excited. I said that I would miss talking with him on Fridays.

Every so often I thought about Paul, assuming that life was good for him and his family. To my surprise, I received a call from him one July morning. He was in town with his family and asked if he could come over to meet me in person. I was pleased to hear from him again. We set up a time for him to drop by between my advising appointments.

A little while later, in came Paul with his wife Donna and his son Brian. All three lined up to hug me as if I were an old friend. Paul and I talked about his new job and his future. Donna and Brian produced a camera and insisted on taking pictures of Paul and me. We posed for several shots under the framed diploma that we have hanging in our outer office, making quite a spectacle as students entered and left their advising appointments.

The moral of the story is this: Every morning as I walk into my office, I tell myself that I am going to try to make a positive difference for someone that day. Most of the differences that we make are small, and many are not even discernable at the time. The story of Paul reminds me that we *do* make differences. Most of us have a "Paul" story tucked away.

These are the stories that bolster us while we meet everyday challenges and commit ourselves to treating each student with the "highest degree of importance."

Louise M. Land

Marcia Kennard Kiessling

Louise M. Land was the first union director I ever met. She was not an expert presenter or facilitator, although she was very capable. I don't know if she was up on the latest student development theories, although I suspect she was. I cannot speak of her specific skill set. I can, however, tell you of her character, because that is how I felt her impact and how she touched the lives of students. Years ago, I was one of those students.

Louise was my best career role model. As an undergraduate student, I was positively influenced by this elderly lady at a time when role models did not come easily to young women seeking careers. By observing and interacting with her, I shaped my vision of what it meant to be a student affairs administrator. I saw that it meant welcoming new people and new ideas, developing relationships built on trust and respect, and having a love for life and for work. It meant encouraging student leaders and being patient as another new batch of students came along, year after year. It meant having a sincere interest in both the life and work of the students. It also meant being truthful, dependable, and reliable. Louise was all these things and more. She was a steady presence, a positive force, and an encourager of students. She was both role model and mentor.

Most evenings, Louise would take her dog for a walk around the perimeter of the campus. She and her husband lived in a house owned by the university. I don't remember an evening that Louise didn't stop by with her dog to check in with the students who were either running programs or managing the union for the evening. She always inquired about the events and listened with sincere interest as we shared our updates.

Time went by, as it always does. Louise retired and I graduated. We stayed in touch. After retirement, Louise went back to school and earned her doctorate. She was very proud of this accomplishment. I clearly saw how it invigorated her. It's funny how people can impact us in ways that we understand only years later. I am not yet retired, but I am now working on my doctoral degree. Seeing Louise obtain her degree was what gave me the initial drive to pursue mine.

If I could sum up in one word what made Louise so special, I would choose the word *encouragement*. This is what Louise did on a regular basis. I believe encouragement is what students and young professionals really need. Louise served for many years formally as union director and informally as role model and mentor. She helped her students discover their worth and how to contribute. Through her daily interactions and her authentic way of being, which at its core was embodied by encouragement, Louise made her greatest contribution.

Reality at Midnight

Carol A. Lundberg

It was 11:30 p.m., much too late to check my inbox, but I wanted to get a glimpse of what had developed in the evening so I could prepare for what I would face the next morning. With e-mail access constantly at my fingertips, I can let my work creep into all the corners of my life, even at home. Setting my better judgment aside, I grabbed the mouse and clicked. A quick glimpse showed a message from Chelsea, a student who was disappointed with a grade she received in my class. She had never earned a C, couldn't bear the thought of earning a C, and she was upset. So was I. I was disappointed that she did not participate fully in the class despite my persistent nudges for deeper learning. Had she paid attention to the syllabus and the way her points were adding up throughout the course, the C would have been no surprise. Thus, I braced myself to stand firm against her grade appeal.

Reading further in her e-mail, I learned of her disappointment, of doubts that she could contribute anything of value to the field of student affairs. This is the conversation we should have had months earlier, the dialogue that would have helped me to make stronger connections between course content and its relevance to her life. My attempts to plunge her deeper into the course material seemed to be meaningless, but my e-mail with the grade C grabbed her attention immediately.

After wallowing in my self-righteous grading policy, I fired an e-mail back. My midnight response caught her also at the computer, so she responded quickly with an offer of a fuller version of the story if I could stay online. Soon, I was reading the unabridged explanation of her semester with me. She told of a supervisor whose expectations she could neither understand nor meet. She described her young son who needed his mommy to tuck him in, but a job that kept her out at meaningless student meetings too many nights. From the safety of her home, wrapped in her bathrobe, she told a story that would never have occurred face to face. Bolstered by the freedom to communicate at her own pace, to craft her words carefully before sending them, Chelsea could tell the real story. I began to soften. Softening doesn't mean changing a grade, nor does it mean lowering the bar for an overwhelmed student. It means listening and trying to understand. Her story was not about the grade or the course, but about an unraveling career in a field for which she was about to earn an advanced degree. My course was necessary in that fruitless pursuit. She described a difficult patch of life, one for which this basement-level grade seemed to be the final blow. I wondered how many other stories impact my classroom, but never make it there in an overt way.

In retrospect, I now see earlier hints of Chelsea's self-doubt, of questioning whether this field was right for her. As a student in our intensive program for full-time professionals, Chelsea came to us with several years of experience in the field of student affairs, seeking the degree she needed to continue her upward mobility. I assumed she enjoyed her work as much as I do. However, my love for this field is a bit like my love for my children: It causes me to overlook elements that are less than ideal, and it hinders other people from telling me about them. In every parent–teacher conference, I expect the teacher to expound upon my unusually wonderful child who can do no wrong. In like manner, I expect my graduate students to see all the opportunity, joy, and satisfaction that I've enjoyed in student affairs for the past 20 years. It may be difficult for them to tell me of a more gloomy view.

I have learned some tricks of getting at the real story with my own kids. If we need to discuss sex or homework, these conversations occur more readily in the car on the way to volleyball practice or to another innocuous event. No one expects eye contact, and we can pretend it is a lighthearted conversation, a subtext to our journey. Sometimes I use those strategies with students, encouraging them to ride with me on an errand or to walk across campus with me. Conversations en route can be a safe place for them to reveal the bigger picture and for me to see their lives more fully. My midnight e-mail conversation reminded me that online communication can be a similar kind of tool, one where the barrier of the computer creates enough safety for the truth to be told. Teachers are sometimes granted glimpses of this truth, snippets of an autobiography that hint at more than we see in the polished veneer of our students. Those stories help us teach the real student, the one with needs, questions, even doubts.

Teachers have a thin veneer, also. When a student doesn't seem to care about my course, it rattles me. I fear that I have shortchanged both student and subject. Sometimes student disinterest prompts me to work harder and listen more. Other times it leads me to pull back, blame students, and polish my perfect-teacher veneer.

Fortunately, Chelsea didn't give up on me. She persisted until I could set aside my defensiveness and hear what she was saying. We finally had the discussions we should have been having all along, discussions about work and family, about trying to be what a supervisor needs, about caring for oneself while caring for others. Most important, we talked about following her heart, even if it led her down a different road than my heart had led me. She ended up switching to an area of student affairs that fit her better, where she felt she could bring her whole self to the job, where she could be home with her son nearly every evening. I hope I gave her the freedom to leave the field entirely, that I supported her in doing whatever she needed to do. If not, maybe she'll e-mail at midnight with a message hinting at discontent. Hopefully, I'll catch on more quickly this time around.

Putting the "Student" Back Into "Student Development"

Elizabeth M. Miller

A ll too frequently as professionals in student affairs, we use the term "student development" to beef up resumes, impress our grandmothers, and, above all, give purpose to our work. At no other time was the term so embedded in my mind as in graduate school, when every student encounter became an opportunity to improve myself and become a better educator. I was, after all, in pursuit of being the best student affairs practitioner of all time. Although it is a hard term to define succinctly, at the time I understood "student development" to be a process that entailed understanding where students were in their personal development and guiding them to a higher understanding of themselves by providing resources, experiences, and support.

It was during my graduate program that I had one of my first "ah ha" moments in student affairs, in which I realized that student development is much more than a process—it is also a value that must be internalized for a practitioner to be a true student affairs professional. This moment occurred during my first fieldwork experience in graduate school, while coordinating a new leadership program at a community college. Although I had been working professionally in the field for a couple years, this assignment was in a different setting and challenged me to work with a new student population. Being a type-A personality who finds comfort in organization, I gave careful attention to the structure, content, and assessment of all my workshops and programs. I spent a lot of time planning student meetings to ensure a learning environment.

During a follow-up session with a student who recently had attended a leadership workshop, I realized that while planning an amazing curriculum with an agenda related to specific student development outcomes is great, too much planning can backfire. I met with "Joe" to discuss how he felt about his leadership skills and abilities, and to discuss the results of a leadership inventory he took at the workshop. I planned a great encounter that focused on his leadership strengths and opportunities for growth, what the inventory measures meant to him, and how to further his skills and abilities by setting goals. As we began the meeting, I was pumped and excited to help him in his student development.

THE MEETING BEGAN

Although new to the office, I had frequently observed Joe interacting with the students, taking an active role in the college's student government, and generally serving as a resource to others. He shared his thoughts on leadership. He reported recognizing few strengths and many areas for improvement. It turned out that Joe was having a hard time at his job. At 17 years old, he felt that his coworkers did not respect him. He was hurt and angry that his supervisor was seemingly aware but uncaring about how he felt. Joe did not respect his company and was experiencing cognitive dissonance with wanting to perform at his best, yet finding himself not wanting to do so for this company.

I realized that discussing the leadership workshop was out of the question. Instead, I drew upon my counseling skills to allow Joe to talk about how he was feeling and how it affected him and his view of himself. Through the discussion I was able to focus on the great leadership skills he exhibited in the senate and showed him that even if his current work situation did not allow him to use his skills directly now, he was building resources within him that were transferable. Helping Joe see the amazing abilities he already had helped build his confidence. We discussed how to view his job as a learning experience. After discussing his goals of being an entrepreneur, I suggested that he perform informational interviews with business owners he respected and connected him with a colleague in a program that mentors business students. I was surprised when Joe got tears in his eyes. I could clearly feel the sense of relief he had when he realized his current situation was only temporary. As our meeting concluded, he was smiling and energetic. I again saw the familiar driven and enthusiastic student.

To this day, I use that experience as a reminder of the importance of being a partner with our students in the learning process and never putting my role as an educator on a pedestal. Having education and experience in student affairs serves as an excellent foundation for my work, but this incident reinforced my belief that hearing a student's story and being adaptive to his or her needs are equally important. I can plan student development as a process and experience, but first I must hold it as a value. Student development yearns to be flexible and adaptive, and trying to cage it as a simple process will stifle its abilities. While I still love structure and planned outcomes, this experience highlighted the fact that the unexpected learning outcomes are often the most meaningful and significant. By putting the "student" back into "student development," and thinking on my feet, I came to understand the value behind the term and the impact it can have on a student's life.

A Young Man and His Mentor

Samuel R. Lopez Jr.

*"The function of education is to teach one to think intensively
and to think critically....Intelligence plus character—that is
the goal of true education."*
—Dr. Martin Luther King Jr.

My life is similar to a kaleidoscope. According to Webster's dictionary, a kaleidoscope "signifies the fragments that come together to form a whole, perhaps indicating a diversity of something, such as experiences, or piecing together the parts of a symbolic puzzle." Growing up on the streets of New York, I have had critical interactions with many different kinds of people and learned important things that make me the man I am today. Every encounter, the good and the bad, taught me important life lessons.

I grew up in Spanish Harlem with both parents and my two little sisters. My father was the superintendant of the building, and my mother stayed home. My father was an alcoholic and my mother a drug user. I remember times when my mother would be unfaithful to my father and inject herself with heroin. I remember going into drug houses and watching her shoot up. I will never forget her glassy eyes. It was strange to see my mother sticking a needle in her arm right in front of me with no remorse. I felt like a seeing eye dog, guiding my mother back to our apartment. My parents were killed for owing drug money to a notorious drug dealer. From that point forward, I was raised on the streets.

I was 8 when my parents died. My sisters were taken by the Administration for Children's Services. I decided to be a runaway and roamed the streets of New York with people I thought were my mother's friends. During that period in my life, I sold drugs and worked as a drug mule. I was separated from my sisters for almost 2 years and spent most of my time afraid. Once, my life flashed right before my eyes when one of my mother's suppliers put a gun to my face and robbed me.

I started living in group and foster homes. I began living in the Bronx with a Dominican family that had two foster kids. Even with an already full home, they added three more children. My sisters and I were reunited when I was 11. This is where we met Dulce, which means "sweet" in Spanish. She gave my sisters and me a sense of hope that we would be a happy family. She also had a set of rules we lived by. She told us that education was very important and that we would earn high school diplomas and college degrees. I realized that I wanted to do well in school and prove to Dulce that education was very important to me, too.

She taught me and my sisters how to cook, do laundry, and wake up by ourselves. She said to me one time in the kitchen, "Sammy, you need to learn to cook. Don't think your wife has to do all the cooking in the house." When Dulce and her husband passed away, I was 18 years old. I felt like I had lost both of my parents again.

My sisters and I moved in with another family whose background was Puerto Rican. Ray and Alida Camacho had two daughters of their own. I was in my last year of high school and about to graduate when we moved in with the Camachos. I was very rebellious. I started cutting class and messing with the wrong people. I also started smoking marijuana. I was on the baseball team, not doing well in my classes. All of this started catching up with me. When my report card came, Alida and Ray called me to their room and asked me to explain what was going on in school. I told them that I was using drugs and did not care about life anymore. They listened to everything that I said, and then they told me, "Sammy, your sisters look up to you. You have to set an example for them and show them that you are the first in the family to graduate. You want them to follow in your footsteps."

I wanted to be a role model for my sisters, somebody they could look up to for advice. I ended up graduating high school, and I was also selected for the all-region baseball team in New York City. I was accepted to John Jay College of Criminal Justice. This is where I met my greatest mentor and my new father, Clayton Walton. He helped me understand the true meaning of helping others. I was a junior in college when I met Mr. Walton and his family. I was working in the office of student activities. They were hiring a new assistant director for the office, and Mr. Walton got the job. I welcomed him to the office. I offered him my assistance because I had worked in the office for several years. I figured I should be the one to help him.

One night, I was working late with Mr. Walton. He told me that he wanted to speak with me. I didn't have a chance to sit down and chat that night because I was running to a student organization meeting. The next day he told me to have a seat in his office. I thought I was fired or he had an issue about my work. Instead, he asked, "What do you want to do with yourself when you graduate? Sammy, you have a talent and you need to use it." He said that I was giving 90% to my student organizations and only 10% to my school work. He pushed me to change the way I balanced school and activities. He showed me that administrators like him would help me, but that I needed to stay focused on school. Mr. Walton was very serious. He told me that he would be all over me if I did not do what I needed to do with the books. This was the tough love that I needed.

He taught me a lot of life lessons. He was more of a father to me than my boss. He taught me how to be a good father by the example that he set with his own children. Mr. Walton considered me to be a part of his family. He showed me a different side of life that I had never experienced growing up as a first-generation student with no stable family. He also shared with me the importance of being a good friend and that he would do his best to be a positive role model.

He was also the one who encouraged me to go to graduate school, and he gave me a strong support network. I feel so happy when I do well in graduate school and tell him, because I have somebody with whom I can share my accomplishments. He tells me I am doing better in grad school then he did as a student. That makes me feel good.

The most important thing that Mr. Walton shared with me: "You have been through a lot of things that not a lot of people have been through. You have beaten all of the obstacles that have been put in front of you. If you can do that, you can do anything." I am no longer afraid to share my story. All of the positive and negative experiences of my life frame this kaleidoscopic image. There have been many experiences, many people, and many insights. Thank you, Clayton, for believing in me and seeing a potential in me that I didn't know I had. Knowing that I have somebody who looks out for me means a lot, but having someone whom I can call "Dad" is priceless.

FLY BUTTERFLY

"Leaf" Yi Zhang

"What should I do?" the girl asked herself. Sitting alone on a bench in the middle of the campus, she avoided eye contact when a few students passed by. She was looking up to the sky, and her eyes welled with tears. This was the most beautiful season on campus. The wind shook the trees, making their colorful leaves dance before the world as cotton-white clouds floated by. However, her heart was not as beautiful as the fall. Rather, her world was the ominous rain cloud: cold, dark, and damp. She was overwhelmed with her course work. She did not know how to make new friends. She did not understand why her classmates laughed when she spoke English. She felt like a failure.

"Am I really a failure?" She couldn't hold her tears back any longer. Hot streaks ran down her cheeks. As a first-generation college student from China, she worked diligently to exceed the requirements and over-came many difficulties to pursue her master's degree in the United States. She thought she would fulfill her dreams and realize her family's hope, but the fact was that she did not even know how to start her new life.

A tissue appeared. She raised her head and found before her a white-haired lady. She was in her late 60s, wearing a navy blue skirt with white trim that rested just above her ankles, a white angora sweater that fit snugly on her skinny frame. Draped around her shoulders was a cream-colored shawl.

"May I sit here?"

She nodded.

"Are you a new student?"

She nodded again.

"Have some problems?"

She nodded a third time.

Waiting for the girl to dry her tears, the lady said, "I guess you want to know someone with more reason to cry." The girl looked at her, puzzled. "It is me." The lady answered with a delightful tone.

"I cried when I was rejected by the best college in my hometown. I cried when I failed the final test of my French course. I cried when in my first job my boss gave me a horrible annual review. I cried when my company told me my division was laid off." She stopped and laughed. "I've cried a lot in my life." Enlightened by the way she told the story, the girl was laughing as well.

"So...." The girl hesitated to ask what happened to her life.

"But I never gave up!" While the white-haired lady was saying this, her face brightened. "Yes, I was declined by the best college, but I prepared for one more year and was accepted by another four-year university. I failed my French course, but I spent more time, and I'm now able to read French texts like it was my native language. I had basically been told I was a lousy employee, but I learned lessons and became one of the best employees there 3 years later. I lost my job as an accountant, but soon I found out my real career interest is to work with students."

Intrigued by the lady's story, the girl started to share her own. "I am a new student in communication studies. My English is *bad*. I don't understand the class. I have *no* friends. I don't want to give up, but I feel I am a failure and I feel I cannot do anything." The girl almost cried again.

Without a word, the lady stood up, took off her shawl, and put it on the girl's shoulders. Holding the girl's arms and looking at her straight in the eye, she said firmly, "Close your eyes and think of all the negative things that you don't like." Puzzled, the girl did so. "Okay, open your eyes when you are ready." Slowly the girl opened her eyes, still puzzled. The old lady took off the shawl and then suddenly tore it apart. "I am just tearing down all the barriers, all the bad things. Join me! You are released from your own 'cocoon' now. Fly freely! Believe in yourself! You can do it!"

"I can do it?"

"You can do it!"

"I can do it!"

"Yes, you can do it!"

The girl's confidence was lit up again. She and the lady shouted to the sky, cheering and celebrating.

In 2 years, the girl, who was flying beautifully without the restrictions of her "cocoon," successfully completed her master's at the university. She asked the lady—who had become her mentor and who turned out to be an associate dean of student affairs—if her story really happened the way she told it at their first meeting. The lady just smiled and said, "*Your* story is more important." The girl, currently pursuing her doctoral degree in higher education, decided to write down this story. She hopes to become someone like her mentor, an education practitioner who has the power to free "butterflies."

President, You Make Everything "Groovy"

Sheila Bustillos Reynolds

During my undergraduate years, I was the president of the Presidential Ambassadors group, a part of the university's development division. To do something for our president on President's Day, the executive council and I decided to bake her favorite red velvet cake and deliver it to her office. I mentioned how interesting it would be if I could write her a song we could all sing while I played my guitar. I was shot down immediately and slightly teased.

So, on President's Day (which landed on a day I had guitar class), we delivered the cake to her office. Seeing the guitar in my hand, the president asked if I was going to play a song. In hindsight, I think she was just trying to make conversation, but I expressed my excitement to play for her. I opened my guitar and searched for an appropriate song to play. I wasn't very good and didn't know many songs. The only one I could think of was the song we played in class that day: "Wild Thing"! Without thinking it through, I started playing the song and improvised the lyrics to fit the President's Day theme. The president was kind and patient while listening to my bad attempt at music.

When we left the office, everyone broke out in laughter and talked in disbelief about my impromptu actions. In retrospect, this story taught me several lessons: (1) students can act on impulse, so be patient with them and let them learn from their mistakes or embarrassments; (2) always be prepared; (3) never play "Wild Thing" to the president of your university, no matter how cleverly you change the lyrics; and (4) take note of the actions of the president—always find time to laugh!

From Thief to Chief: How a Dean's Approach Inspired an Irresponsible College Student

Ty Patterson

On a beautiful Sunday early in May 1964, I was playing poker at a friend's apartment when the dean of men found me. To this day I have no idea how. Dean Webber was a stern man with a speech as measured as his voice was gravelly. He merely said, "Come with me!" There was no other option. Not a word was spoken during the 10-minute ride back to campus that seemed to take forever. I knew where I'd gotten the money to finance the gambling, and I was afraid Dean Webber knew, too. I had stolen eight textbooks from students, crossed their names out and put in mine, and turned them in for cash at the student union bookstore. This inept larceny generated about $60, enough to buy beer for a few days and finance my gambling. When we got to campus, Dean Webber took me straight to his office. I believe it is no exaggeration to say what transpired in the next hour or so changed my life forever.

It is impossible for me to remember the details of that meeting, but I'll never forget the way Dean Webber treated me that afternoon. He was kind but firm. Above all, he treated me with genuine respect. He knew a lot about me: where I was from, the names of my parents, the kind of scholarship I'd received, and that I was about to flunk out. We talked about what was happening in my life. He listened. Then he kicked me out of school. He gave me a check for $60 from the dean of men's loan fund on the condition I immediately find and repay, in person, the students from whom I'd stolen the books. He called my parents to let me explain, in front of him, what happened. As I walked away from his office, all I could think was, "I wish someday I could do what he does for a living."

That fall, I received permission to continue college on academic probation. After a month, I could see that I was not ready for college. I withdrew and joined the U.S. Air Force. Serving in the military helped me grow up. The opportunity to travel and meet people from different backgrounds was an education in itself; so, too, was the experience of the war in Viet Nam. In 1968, I received an honorable discharge and returned to the United States from Southeast Asia. I decided to "return to the scene of the crime" and enrolled again in January 1969. I was hired as a peer academic advisor in a brand new program called Guidance and Academic Advisement Services. That was my first taste of what was to become a career of serving students.

In June 2008, I retired as vice president of student services at Ozarks Technical Community College in Springfield, Missouri. Over 30 years, I served as chief student services officer in three community colleges. Through those years, I had the opportunity to kick a lot of students out of college. Every time, I thought about the way Dean Webber treated me and tried my best to follow his example.

In the way he responded to my behavior, Dean Webber taught me how to make a difference in someone's life when he or she is in trouble. He demonstrated the satisfaction one can derive from holding someone accountable for their actions. Thank goodness Dean Webber saw the opportunity in his interaction with an irresponsible college student such a long time ago.

A Second Chance

Megan A. Stone

Sometimes in the midst of my hectic day, I sit down and reflect. As a second-year graduate student in a college student personnel program, I often think back to the experiences in my life that helped me commit to this particular career path. It is important to have passion for a chosen career. I often use my experiences to help motivate my purpose and philosophy. When I reflect on the reason I chose my graduate major, I think back to the summer before my freshman year and the 5 years that followed.

It was July 2002, the summer before I began my freshman year at Virginia Tech. I was excited to find out that I had received a scholarship to play softball, and I was working hard the summer before to try to stay in shape. I was determined to be the best I could be in both academics and athletics. That summer, I remember getting sick with a horrible fever and headache. I started feeling a heaviness in my chest. I insisted on playing my softball games, even though I felt extremely ill. I thought it was a bad cold that I would eventually shake off. I even went to the local hospital, where doctors diagnosed me with bronchial spasms. I thought I was going to be all right in a few days.

July 13, 2002, started out like any ordinary Saturday. Little did I know, the events of that day would profoundly change my life. I was supposed to pitch in a summer league softball game. I really wanted to get back on the pitcher's mound and show everyone what I was made of as a leader and softball player. A discussion with my father and coaches about whether or not I should play made me realize that I was still extremely sick. It was unsafe for me to be out on the softball field in the hot summer weather. I sadly sat down on a picnic table next to my team's dugout and began to watch the game. The next thing I knew, I felt a sharp pain in my heart. I was turning blue. I quickly lost my sight. I was sweating, yet cold to the touch. I had no idea what was happening to me. All I could hear were the screams and cries of my teammates and fans sitting on the bench beside the picnic table. I was quickly transported to the nearest hospital for assessment and eventually was returned to the same hospital that diagnosed me with bronchial spasms. Physicians immediately admitted me for further observation.

My vital signs worsened the first night in the hospital. The doctors repeatedly shoved my parents out of the room so they could stabilize me. The doctors did not know what was wrong and gave my family little hope that I would survive the night. My friends and family came into my room to say their goodbyes. Although I was seriously sick, I will never forget their faces and the way they looked at me with extreme sadness.

The night turned into morning, and somehow I survived. I finally stabilized, yet I was not out of the woods. I could only eat ice chips, and the heaviness in my chest seemed to worsen. I felt completely vulnerable and helpless, but I knew that I had to keep fighting or I would die. The doctors finally determined that I had myocarditis. A virus overtook my heart, and my heart began producing copious amounts of fluid to kill off the virus. Consequently, the sac around my heart filled up with fluid and compressed my heart until it no longer pumped, stopping the blood from being transported to my organs.

Since the hospital was unprepared to handle a case of this magnitude, I was quickly transferred to the best cardiac hospital in Pittsburgh. In 11 days, I died numerous times and was brought back, had medical procedures performed I could never fathom being done again, nearly had a heart transplant, and had to learn to walk again because my legs atrophied so badly. Miraculously, after those 11 days, I was discharged from the hospital with only fatigue and the scare of my life. The doctor said that I was a miracle and the worst case he had seen that year.

I knew that college and softball were rapidly approaching, and I had to make a decision whether or not to step onto campus that first day. I was released from the hospital on July 23, 2002. I was to start my freshman year of college the second week of August. I was not sure if I could physically or emotionally start my freshman year, but at the same time, I knew I wanted to continue with my life. College was the next step for me.

The first year of college was definitely an adjustment, especially since I was still so fatigued and my body was recovering from the shock of the entire experience. I remember being scared to be away from my family and friends. I was unsure if I would survive after experiencing something so traumatic. It only took a week to realize that I was in the right place. I was given the support and guidance I desperately needed, while still feeling independent. I played softball that year wearing a heart monitor. I slowly felt the pieces of my life fitting back together. That first year was hard, but despite my trials and tribulations, I knew that I could rely on the staff and administrators around campus to show me the support I needed to flourish. I became a part of a bigger family. I knew that I could lean on my teammates, coaches, and staff across campus if ever I felt overwhelmed or needed to talk. They helped me focus on my goals and how I could achieve them. I became a stronger person after I survived my near-death experience.

From time to time, I reflect on those 11 days in July, and they remind me that one never knows what a student is experiencing. Students may have smiles on their faces while dealing with indescribable situations and life-altering events. This lesson is an extremely important one for me, since I will be working in a higher education institution surrounded by students who might need a pat on the back or a few words of encouragement. It would have been extremely difficult to make it through my freshman year without the support of the staff and administrators in the campus community.

I had such a positive experience as an undergraduate that I wanted to offer students the same support I received. My personal experiences helped me realize my passion and career direction. I value them greatly as I continue my journey within the field of higher education. My near-death experience taught me about compassion and empathy, which I can use as a future professional in the field.

My Name is Sterling!

Kenneth L. Stoner

I have shared this true story of an encounter with a man named Sterling on a number of occasions. Our family involvement with Sterling lasted no more than 15 minutes, at most. The way our paths crossed and the specific encounter was unanticipated, but it is imprinted in my memory as if it were yesterday. There are great lessons to be learned from others who may have no affiliation with any educational institution. I thank Sterling for his insightful instruction. Some 20 years after our encounter, I continue to be awed by the lasting impact this meeting had on a nervous young family.

It was Tuesday, July 2, 1985. I had recently accepted a position as director of student housing, and we scheduled a moving van to relocate us from Tennessee to Kansas. The company indicated they would have one of their drivers/movers meet us at our home at 9:00 a.m. to pack and move the contents.

We were nervous. Before 1985, we had always moved ourselves. But over the years, we had acquired a second car and a pop-up camper, purchased a home, and had two children. It's amazing what a family can accumulate in a few short years. We decided, for the first time in our lives, that we would hire a moving company to relocate us.

No one tells stories of great service from moving companies. The horror stories of broken furniture, lengthy delays in shipping, and missing items weighed heavily on our minds. Our belongings might not have seemed like much to others, but they were *our* belongings—with meaning, sentimental value, and personal attachment. It was a big decision for us. "We were nervous" was an understatement.

In any event, lists were made and special instructions written so we could efficiently and thoroughly communicate important information to the mover. We were ready to say, "Come on in. Let us review this list, walk through the house, and tell you about our belongings. These are important things for you to know."

On the appointed day, a few minutes before 9:00 a.m., the doorbell rang. We were all at the door within seconds. Before we could even utter "come on in," the man at the door immediately said, "Good day, Mr. and Mrs. Stoner. My name is Sterling, and I'm here to move you to Kansas. Come on out for a minute. I want to show you my truck. Bring the kids. I know they'll enjoy seeing a big rig up close." We were speechless. We were ready to pounce on him and say "come on in," but before we could say anything, he said "come on out." Our carefully prepared game plan was instantly disrupted.

We dutifully followed Sterling out to the semitrailer. The side panel was already down with a ramp to the driveway. Sterling walked to the front of the truck and we followed. Looking at any tractor-trailer rig, I have always been impressed by the size of the cab and the implied power of the engine. But this rig was even more remarkable. In addition to the size and power, the entire front end was chrome-plated and sparkled in the morning sun. We could see our faces in it, as if it were a mirror. In large script, angling up from the lower left to the upper right corners across the front of the grill, was written "Sterling." He pointed to the name with pride, and said once again, "That's me. My name is Sterling."

From there, we walked to the side of the truck and up the ramp into the trailer. The compartment had an oak pegged floor that was polished to a shine. The walls were paneled, and there was recessed interior lighting all the way around. The trailer looked as elegant as a formal living room. My wife and I were speechless, while our children asked a myriad of questions, such as "Do you sleep in the truck?" "Have you driven to Alaska?" and "Where did you find the grill with 'Sterling' written on it?" He patiently answered all their questions with a reassuring and comforting smile. We wandered back to the front of the truck to look at the impressive grill. Sterling said,

I know you're nervous. Most families are when it comes to moving. But, as I said, my name is Sterling. I just wanted you to see how I take care of and how I treat my truck. I will take care of and treat your belongings the same way. I do this for a living. And yes, I read the specific instructions you filed with the company, and I will be sure to lock the door when I finish. The best way for you to help me out is to get in your car and head to Kansas and leave the packing and moving to me. Now, Mr. and Mrs. Stoner, I won't lie to you, something could go wrong, but I can guarantee that if something does go wrong, it will not be because I wasn't doing my job or because I didn't care. You have a safe journey, and I'll see you in Kansas next week.

With that, the four of us got into our preloaded vehicle with the pop-up camper in tow and departed with a confidence and comfort that would have been unimaginable an hour earlier. Everything arrived in Kansas on schedule, in the same condition it departed Tennessee. Nothing was broken. Nothing was missing. The delivery was on time. What an experience!

I have thought of that encounter with Sterling many times. Driving on highway or interstates, I occasionally scrutinize oncoming trucks or look in the rearview mirror to see if I can catch a glimpse of that grill with "Sterling" across the front. Many times, my children would turn their heads as we passed trucks that bore the same company logo as the one for which Sterling hauled. Sometimes I would ask, "What are you looking for?" Invariably, the answer was, "Just checking to see if that might be Sterling!" Our children are now 26 and 32, both college graduates, married, and gainfully employed. But even today, the topic of "I wonder where Sterling is?" still comes up on occasion.

As time passed and my career in the university environment continued to evolve, I often recalled this instructive encounter with Sterling. I have specifically recounted the story when I have challenged staff to develop ways to immediately convey personal acceptance and understanding, as well as our professional commitment to our students and to their parents and others who care for them.

We know the nervousness of families and their children. Although each of us works with hundreds of students, we know there is tremendous personal ownership attached to the individuality and value of each person attending our institutions that far exceeds the feelings associated with belongings and property. We know that families are concerned that their loved ones are moving outside the immediate safety net they have carefully and intentionally woven over the years. We know that leaving a loved one in the hands of people who are unknown is difficult. We know it is important to immediately address these concerns through our new student orientation sessions, through our parents associations, through our residential life programs, and through our other activities and interactions with parents and families. We know that for every student, college attendance is a once-in-a-lifetime journey that will be a point of demarcation and a place of reference for their respective futures. We know that occasionally something can go wrong, but we are also committed to ensuring that it will not be because "we were not doing our jobs" or because "we didn't care." We know what we are doing and are prepared to shepherd our students along on their unique educational journeys. We are aware and understand the nervousness.

With each and every encounter, our challenge is to insert our own name for Sterling's and say with reassurance and confidence, "Good day, my name is Sterling; I am here to move you to graduation."

A Circuitous Calling into Student Affairs

Rishi Sriram

My journey into higher education and student affairs had an unusual beginning. In my first year as an undergraduate student, I felt I was the only person among my peers who did not have his or her life mapped out. My friends not only had selected their respective majors and minors, but also had strategic plans projecting them into the next several decades. So, when I was asked by my fellow students to reveal my major, it was with a fair amount of embarrassment that I would explain I was undecided. "Undecided" felt like a substitute word for "unintelligent." Surely anyone who was bright, made good grades, and had any drive to be successful would, at a minimum, know what major to select. How could I claim those things if I had no clue what my future vocation should be?

I was, therefore, overcome with a great sense of simultaneous gratitude and relief when my English professor invited me to her house for lunch one Saturday and talked to me about the possibility of selecting English as my major. She saw potential. I saw an opportunity to simultaneously make my professor happy and get the proverbial monkey off my back. Shortly after deciding to major in English, I began to seriously consider working toward becoming an English professor. I loved college students, and the idea of working with them, teaching them, and learning from them quickened my spirit.

It is somewhat ironic, then, that my dream of becoming an English professor was thrown off course during lunch with another professor a few years later. He was a faculty member in the business school and had befriended me after we connected through a mutual acquaintance. When I told him I wanted to become an English professor, I did not expect him to question me. After all, he was a professor himself! But true friends ask the difficult questions. When he asked me why I wanted to become a faculty member in English, my answers were quick and to the point. I loved college students and wanted to work with them. In a very gentle but firm way, my friend explained to me that the road to the professoriate would be very difficult. I would not survive it if I did not have a passion for the discipline of English that equaled or exceeded my passion for college students.

It was a difficult conversation, but one that showed me that I settled for an easy answer to the question of my vocation. Some answers cannot come that easily. I felt as though I was back at square one, in a desperate panic to figure out what I should do with my life. I was just months away from graduation, and the days were passing by like minutes. My desperation reached such a high point that I resorted to sitting on my bed and flipping through the university course catalogue to search for any possible graduate programs that might interest me. I had no idea, until that moment, of the existence of student affairs as a profession— a graduate program designed for people who wanted to work with college students!

My graduate program not only enriched my mind, but also shifted my paradigm of student affairs as a profession. I quickly learned that student affairs is not simply a touchy-feely, hang-out-with-college-students kind of field. I certainly get to build relationships with students, and there are many moments when my heart is filled, but I seriously underestimated the intellectual competence needed to be a student affairs professional. Systems thinking, student development theories, and research practices thrust me into a new, wonderfully challenging world. I learned that shaping the future citizens and leaders of our world is no small calling.

I spent the next several years completing my master's degree in higher education and obtaining my first position working with college students. I enjoyed the work immensely. I felt closer to my vocational calling than ever before in my life. I also felt as though something was missing. I had a desire to discover in more depth what environments and programs actually help students learn and develop better. Therefore, I decided to pursue a PhD in higher education and continue my journey in learning what it means to be a scholar of higher education.

Fortunately, my PhD program required students to take a course on teaching and learning. It was during this course that everything began to come together, almost circuitously. We explored what it means to teach and to learn as we discussed the writings of various scholars, such as Robert Barr, John Tagg, and Parker Palmer. For the first time, I could begin to see how the events of the past were not random collisions of nature, but rather stops and turns on the same continuing journey. I originally wanted to be a professor because I loved the idea of working with college students. I later began to see that studying college students has become a discipline in itself. Now I saw an opportunity to one day teach, mentor, and develop the future leaders of higher education.

I currently have the opportunity to teach an undergraduate leadership course and participate as students discover how their talents can contribute to a more just and humane world. The opportunity to teach this course is a gift that I cherish each semester. I am always surprised by how much I learn from the students. As we journey together in class, I share my profession, wondering if any of them have the potential and passion for student affairs.

I am also privileged to directly work with nine faculty-in-residence who come from a wide range of disciplines. These faculty members are full partners with and advocates for student affairs. They invite me into dialogue about pedagogy that transcends their individual disciplines toward the universal goal of student learning.

The thought of being a professor who studies college students never crossed my mind as an undergraduate. Now I'm journeying toward that vocation. The timing could not be better. There is so much to learn about how college students best develop, especially those college students who have been traditionally underrepresented.

It may have taken me 10 years to discover my "major," but I believe I finally found it. I'm thankful for the two professors who took the time to sit down with me and talk about my future. This is my vocation, but I do not think I'm alone. The challenge for student affairs is that, unlike many other graduate programs, there is no undergraduate major directly connected to what we do. Television shows dramatize and glorify professions such as business, medicine, and law, but it is doubtful that student affairs will ever have that kind of visibility. Yet we desperately need talented women and men who devote themselves to making significant contributions to the field of higher education through research, writing, teaching, and developing the future leaders of our colleges and universities. If only someone will take the time to sit down with our best and brightest students and suggest it.

I Think He's Going to Kill Me

Penny Rice

The Sloss House was built in 1883 and, as the women's center at the university, has provided a safe haven for students, staff, and faculty. Staff offices are located in the former tiny bedrooms on the second floor of the house. The house itself is tiny, which adds to the sense of safety and warmth. It is difficult for someone to enter the front door and climb the steps to our offices without making the floorboards creak.

Just before midterm of the semester, things start to settle down slightly in my office. I take advantage of this time to put files away and sort through piles of mail. The day I met Danielle started out like any other in the women's center. There were a number of telephone calls that needed to be returned and numerous e-mails waiting for my response, and I was preparing for a supervisory meeting.

Our secretary was at her desk just outside my office with a student when we all heard the front door slam and feet running up the stairwell. Danielle entered the office hyperventilating as she sobbed, "I think he's going to kill me!" My secretary immediately swept Danielle into my office.

After giving her tissues and a glass of water, I waited for Danielle to calm down enough to speak. As she caught her thoughts and breath, I asked her if she was safe right now. She nodded her head. Danielle told me her story, beginning at the end. "He's going to kill me. He keeps beating me, and each time it gets worse. I don't think I'm going to live through the week."

Danielle moved to Ames from a small Iowa town. She and her boyfriend decided to break up, since he planned on staying home and they would be 3 hours away from each other. Danielle moved into the residence halls and had a wonderful time meeting new people and attending class. Three weeks into the semester, her boyfriend surprised her by showing up on campus. He had an apartment and a job, and wanted her to move in with him. She hesitated because she really enjoyed the people on her floor, but she thought she loved him and should move in.

"I was scared from the minute I stepped into his apartment. He started calling me all sorts of horrible names and accusing me of sleeping with other guys. It was just awful. I knew I couldn't get out of there by myself. Most of the friends I made I didn't know well enough to share this with, so I stayed. He would take me to class and wait for me to finish. The only relief I got was when he was at work. Even then he would call every 5 minutes to find out where I was and what I was doing. The last time he beat me, I blacked out. I don't know how long I was out. I think I should see a doctor, but I'm terrified that he'll find out. He was verbally abusive when we were in high school and always controlled my time. There was one time that he shoved me so hard I fell down because he was upset that I was late coming out of class."

We discussed several options for Danielle, contacted the county domestic violence shelter, and developed an escape plan together. She made a few phone calls to family and friends from home to ask for their help moving. Then we discussed her academics. Danielle was not doing well in any of her classes and didn't think she could get it together fast enough to do well her first semester. The escape plan expanded to include a complete withdrawal from school.

Danielle left my office much calmer and somewhat confident. I wrote down several numbers for her to contact to complete her withdrawal, room release, and exit from the university. We talked with each office during our meeting, and they knew she would be in touch in the next 2 days. As she hugged me and thanked me for my help, I fought the desire to scoop her up and take her home. I fought back my own tears and asked her if she would let me know how she is doing.

Danielle left and I returned to my office sobbing. Danielle was the same age as my own daughter, 18 years old. She was just starting to find and live out her dream. There was no way to know what would come next for this young woman. The police would help her remove her belongings from the apartment, but even with a protective order, women are still killed by men who say they love them. I was terrified.

Danielle withdrew from the university and returned home for a short time. But home wasn't safe either, because he returned home, too. She ended up finding a job and living with a friend out of state for a year, and started working with a counselor. She transferred to a different school that, she said, "didn't have any memories of him." She sent me letters, e-mails, and cards that always started with, "I don't know if you'll remember me or not, but I came in your office for help one day."

Danielle finished college and is working in the social work field. She is a confident, strong survivor. I will never forget the moment I met her and am forever grateful to have had the opportunity to support and assist her when she asked for help. Too many women experience this violence alone.

The inspiration I hope you take from this story is that as student affairs professionals, we must learn to assist and support all students, no matter the circumstances they present to us. We must become aware of the early signals of relationship violence and do everything we can to help students overcome the horrors of their past and present while preparing for their future.

Girls Like to Swim

Georgia Pullen

It was the Sunday of Labor Day weekend when I received a call from plant facilities.

"The pool in one of the student suites on the third floor is leaking into the suite below." Tom, being a nuts-and-bolts kind of guy, was not known for his personable nature or his sense of humor, especially on the Sunday of Labor Day weekend.

"A pool?"

"Yes, a pool."

"A *kiddie* pool?"

"No, a 13' × 3' foot pool complete with an aluminum ladder to get in and out. It was only filled about a quarter of the way, thank goodness, or the pool would be *in* the second floor suite!"

The following Tuesday, three young men marched into my office. I affectionately refer to them as "the swimming team." They smiled and sat down in a rather nonchalant, without-a-care-in-the world manner. I returned their smile. After some silence, I asked them to explain to me just exactly what they were thinking when they converted one of the rooms in the suite into a Bahaman getaway.

The captain of the team spoke first: "Girls like to swim—especially in North Dakota and especially in the fall and winter. We thought it would be a chick magnet. Great way to meet girls, don't you think?" Receiving no response, he continued. "After all, your handbook doesn't say we can't have a pool. We didn't break any rules."

"You are so correct," I responded. "In the 105-year history of this fine institution, this is a first. As a college student, however, I would think you would have deduced that since one cannot have an aquarium over 10 gallons, a pool would probably be prohibited."

I asked them to figure out how heavy the pool would be had they managed to fill it before they left for the weekend. They figured out that it would be "29,000 or so pounds." I asked if they believed the floor would hold that kind of weight.

The captain said, "We were very safety-conscious. We covered all the electrical outlets with duct tape. We didn't want anyone to get electrocuted."

"Thank you for that, but again, would the floor have held that kind of weight?"

"No?" he questioned.

"No, I think not. What caused the leak anyway?"

"Evidently, we accidentally punctured the bladder when we were setting the stakes. It wasn't easy to get it all into that small room," he lamented.

Realizing that this might be a good scenario for restorative justice, I asked, "Who do you think was harmed by your actions?"

The second team member answered, "Well, no one really. We know we have to pay for the damages to the floor and ceiling, but other than that, no one was harmed."

I smiled. "What did you boys do for the Labor Day weekend?" One went to the lake with his family; one went home to the farm; one went camping with friends.

"Who do you think had to clean up your mess? Who do you think had to give up Sunday and Monday of Labor Day weekend to repair the floor and ceiling?"

"The custodian?"

"No, the supervisor, who, by the way, does not get paid by the hour but is on salary, which means he had to leave his family and friends and work for absolutely nothing."

I stared and no one spoke for what seemed to be an eternity. Finally, the team captain said, "Maybe we should apologize to him?"

"*Apologize* to him? Oh, I'm thinking that's a given," I retorted.

Silence. The once-nonchalant attitude was slowly giving away to nervous apprehension.

"Maybe we should help him out with his other work?" the captain sheepishly asked.

"That might be a very good idea. You can set that up with him. I'll give you his number before you leave. Who else was harmed?"

Again, the silence was deafening, finally broken by the second team member: "Maybe the guy who lives below?"

"Yes, I would think so. Have you contacted him to see what, if anything, was damaged as a result of the pool? Have you bothered to apologize to him for the inconvenience?"

"We can do that, too!" he anxiously responded.

The third team member, who up to this point hadn't said anything, chirped up. "I live in the suite, but I didn't pay for the pool. It was $400, and I couldn't help pay for it. I didn't help them set it up. I didn't fill it. I didn't cover the outlets or hang the posters. I knew it was wrong. I shouldn't get in any trouble at all. It was these guys. Not me."

His teammates got a glimpse of his true colors and were obviously annoyed. I said, "Did you stop them or report it? When the girls showed up, I suppose you would have gone into your room, shut the door, and had nothing to do with the party? Are you telling me that?"

No comment.

I turned to the other two and said, "Now you gentlemen know what it's like to be hung out to dry." I turned to the defector and said, "You need to think about what it means to take responsibility for your actions or, in your case, lack of action, which—don't ever forget—is the same as consent."

I find that students are often much harder on themselves when they are held accountable. Restorative justice, when appropriate, is preferable to traditional sanctions. To this day, the "swimming team" stops in for a few laughs, because the outcome was a positive learning experience for all.

The two team members were good as their word. They donated the pool, the ladder, the pump, and the posters to the campus auction. They met with the student downstairs who, in my opinion, let them off rather lightly. But then there was the custodial supervisor. He definitely enjoyed working with these gentlemen—or rather, watching these gentlemen work. As far as what happened with the third student, that's another story!

A GROWNUP ON THE INSIDE

NATALIE PAGEL

Growing up as the fourth of five children, independent was never a term used to describe me. When our family would pile into our old station wagon to go somewhere, I never asked questions—I just followed everyone else. I attended college in my hometown, studying French. I knew it wasn't a particularly pragmatic major, but I loved everything about it: The ability to connect with someone in their language and to understand their culture excited me. It wasn't so much the ability to read and speak the French language itself that I loved—although it was beautiful—it was the fact that I could communicate with another person outside my world; someone from France, Belgium, or the Ivory Coast.

When I began to entertain the idea of studying abroad, my mother could barely hold back her fears about my leaving to live so far away. Our family had never had the opportunity to visit places like Europe so, in her view, France was an unknown land. My father, drawing from his experience of one week in London, said, "Why d'you want to go there? It's so crowded!" I didn't bother to point out that France was completely different than England. To him, it was all the same: not at home and away from him. I knew that if I wanted to study abroad, I would need financial support in the form of scholarships. I didn't know anything about it. It seemed like a big mountain, and I had only a little spoon to start digging my way through.

On my first visit to the study-abroad office, I met Gerry Auel, the coordinator of exchange programs. She seemed like a very busy woman, always taking phone calls, sending e-mails, and answering questions from the students who constantly formed a line in front of her office. When it was my turn to meet with her, she surprised me with her frank yet gentle manner. Looking back, I think she noticed how determined I was to live in a country that I had never visited. At the end of our conversation, I mentioned the matter that worried me most—money. She encouraged me to apply for a very competitive scholarship offered to study-abroad students. If I got it, it would cover all my expenses. I think she knew that was my only chance.

After several months of working together on my application and researching programs, the unthinkable happened—I received all the funds I needed to study for one year at the Universite de Charles de Gaulle, in Lille, France. Although my family said how proud they were of me, I knew they were worried. My older sister commented, "Natalie, you get lost so easily; how are you going to make it over there?" I had to admit that she was right, but because she always knew the way, I never really had to think about it. I just wanted the chance to do things on my own. At home and in the study-abroad office, it seemed I was two different people. At home, my big family's loving concern made me think twice about what I was doing; at the study-abroad office, I felt that I was an aspiring world traveler and that this was an opportunity of a lifetime. I was both persons—I still felt like a little bird in my family's cozy nest, but Gerry helped me to see that I was growing. As an advisor, she drew out the adult in me, even when I felt I was still a child.

That year was full of so many experiences—even today, memories of situations come to mind that bring a giggle, a sigh, and even a nervous feeling. The process of making two very different educational systems compatible in course descriptions and grades was one of the most challenging tasks I faced. If it hadn't been for Gerry's willingness to coordinate with me and provide the encouragement I needed, I don't know how I would have continued. Gerry made time to have phone appointments with me, despite the 7-hour time difference, listening to my struggles and exciting new experiences, such as my difficulty communicating with my poetry professor or my wild times riding on a bus for 20 hours with the French cross-country team. In a way, she was a bit like a mother, and I wanted to make her proud of me. I felt as though she went above and beyond her professional duties to make my experience worthwhile.

After I returned from France, during my last year of college, Gerry recruited me to help out in the study-abroad office. I found my little niche, helping American students who wanted to study abroad as well as foreign exchange students. I drew on my own experiences abroad to share with students who had just arrived at their new schools and were having a hard time adjusting or understanding teachers in class. As I shared my experiences, I sensed that they felt more comfortable about their adventure. I loved that feeling. Gerry made me feel important every time she suggested that I give advice to aspiring study-abroad students. My involvement in that little office in the basement triggered some major decisions in my life.

I am now pursuing a master's degree in adult and higher education. There's nothing I would enjoy more than helping international students feel at home and helping students who are just like I was venture out and experience a completely different culture. Gerry still works at my alma mater, helping students study abroad and receiving many foreign exchange students. In her mind, I might be just one of her many study-abroad students, but in my mind, she is so much more.

Larger Life Lessons

Kristine Petersen

Nervous small talk filled the airy room. I wore a name tag that identified me as being with the office putting on the workshop, yet I wasn't sure what I had gotten myself into. Around me sat women who varied in age from 20 to 60, and all of them thought I had answers. I certainly didn't think I had any answers. I was just a practicum student for the women's resource center at the local community college. I was here to learn—just like them. Yet they looked to me expectantly at the back-to-school workshop, which they were attending to get the resources and advice they needed to succeed in school. As the workshop began, I thought about how I ended up here in the first place.

In the summer between my first and second years of graduate school, I was offered a practicum opportunity in a women's resource center. Never having considered this area of student affairs, I seized the chance to try something completely different from residence life and programming. My enthusiasm grew once I began the practicum experience, and by the end of my first week at the school, I found myself surrounded by a dozen nontraditional students who had all made the life-altering decision to come to college.

At the beginning of the workshop, each new student introduced herself and told why she decided to come back to school. I wasn't prepared to hear what they had to say. They spoke quietly at first, nervous to tell their stories, not sharing too much. Once a couple women had spoken, the introductions evolved from just their name and some goals to abbreviated versions of their life stories.

"I'm in the process of getting a divorce after being married for more than 30 years. My husband didn't want me to go to college because he liked to be in control. Now I'm ready to take control of my own life."

"People always told me that I was dumb in high school. I believed them for a long time, but I don't think they're right. I want to prove them wrong. I want to have a better life for me and my family."

"I don't have a perfect life. I worked in an adult industry for a long time. One day I woke up and realized that that isn't who I am. I'm coming to find out who I really am and to give my child better options. I want to be a good role model."

As each of the women told her story, my heart ached and my head spun. Higher education was something that was taken for granted in my world. It was assumed that I would go to college after high school. There was no alternative. And that was how it was for almost everyone I knew. So, to hear these women's stories of how they were denied instruction or lived with circumstances that prevented them from getting an education broke my heart. At the same time, I was inspired by their words. Here were some amazing people who were able to overcome so much collectively: divorce, abuse, low self-esteem, early motherhood, and low incomes. So many factors could have kept any of them from enrolling, yet here they were, enrolling in classes and getting information that would help them to be successful students.

At the end of the workshop, I stood up to speak to them. Their stories replayed in my mind, and I gulped as they looked at me. How could my words even compare with what they had shared? I smiled nervously and took a deep breath. "I want each of you to know that you are incredible. I admire you all so much because you've been through so much. Your stories have inspired me and given me hope. Thank you so much. I know that each of you will be successful because of your past. If you can leave an abusive relationship or raise children on your own, then you can graduate from college. You're not in this alone. You will all be successful because you are already successful in so many ways. I wish you nothing but success and joy in your journey through school." Although I had just stood up to merely wish them good luck, I felt that my short speech was necessary. The women in that workshop moved me more than they realized.

Less than 2 months later, I got into an argument with my boyfriend that ended with him attacking me. I managed to escape from the incident with only minor bruises, but major emotional wounds. As I filed the police report, the women's stories played in my mind. I thought of their negative experiences. I thought of the pain they must have endured. More important, though, I thought of their strength and perseverance, of the pride in their eyes as they spoke of better lives and wanting to make positive changes. Instead of sinking into a depression, I drew from their stories, their experiences. I refused to become bitter because of the incident. I knew I could get through this and come out stronger, in part because of the women's stories. They refused to let life get them down. I would follow their example and persevere.

I thanked the students on the day of the workshop because they had inspired me. I wish I could thank them now. Because of them, that day profoundly affected my life. Those women might have been looking at me for information that day, but ultimately they already had the answers to the larger life lesson that I was just learning.

WHEN LIFE SAYS "PAY ATTENTION!"

BOB ORRANGE

O ne spring, my graduate assistant stopped in my office and casually asked if I was going to attend her graduation ceremony. Quite
frankly, I had no intention of going, but only because the ceremony was
on a work day. Our university has at least a half dozen ceremonies every
spring, and as much as I would love to participate, the reality is that as
an administrator, I don't have the luxury of taking time off for each one.
When I told Melissa that I wasn't planning to attend, she replied, "Well,
I'd like you to." With a slight hesitation, I said, "Okay."

I realized that I might be coming across as someone who was not
very empathic. Normally, I'm very much in tune with my students, cli-
ents, and colleagues. My GA had to ask me to attend her ceremony, but
I probably should have planned on going all along. This was going to be
one of the most important moments in her life, and she wanted me to
be there to share it. It was not that I didn't want to attend; it was just
that I was feeling overwhelmed. Besides the normal work-related stress
and being the father of two very young children, my own father was in
failing health and had been recently hospitalized. My family was bracing
for the worst.

The night before the ceremony I, along with the rest of my fam-
ily, visited my father in the hospital for a final goodbye. My dad was a
World War II Navy veteran and, in many ways, a classic member of the
"Greatest Generation." He was my hero—a big, strong, Irish cop from
Buffalo, New York, who always had a twinkle in his eye and a funny
story to tell. He traveled around the world during the war. He loved John
Wayne movies and Bing Crosby songs, but mostly he loved my mom. He

called her "Sug," as in "Sugar." As I was driving his Sug home from the hospital that night, wondering whether I'd ever see my dad alive again, I began to think about Melissa and the promise I'd made to attend her ceremony. She was my GA for 2 full academic years. Smart, dependable, and down to earth, she was the complete package, the kind of colleague you appreciate more and more with each passing year. We had grown from a student-supervisor relationship to something much stronger. I realized that I was going to have to test that relationship, because I decided to skip the ceremony the next day to be with my mom, dad, and the rest of my family. "What's the big deal?" I thought. You sit for a few hours, watch people you don't know march around, while waiting for the one person you do know to walk across the stage. When my phone rang early the following morning with the news that the family was being called back to the hospital to await the inevitable, I jumped in the car knowing that Melissa would understand. "Of course she will," I said to myself. "She is a wonderful, caring person." As I was on my way to the hospital, I had the thought that even though she would understand, she would also be disappointed. I hated that thought. After much internal debate, I finally decided that I could not disappoint her. She had asked me to go and I had agreed. I didn't need to wonder what a certain Irish cop would say about keeping my word.

I drove to the ceremony, telling myself I would make eye contact, wave, and then go to the hospital. There was no way she would know that I did not stay. One problem: Have you ever entered a large, dark auditorium trying to find one person? Did I happen to mention that everyone was wearing the same damn thing? All I could see in every direction were black caps and black gowns!

I went up and down aisles, got in people's way, stepped on toes, looking for my GA. All I could think of was, "What am I doing here? I need to get to the hospital!"

That was when I spotted her. At least I thought it was her. It was hard to tell because she was 200 feet away. The person I spotted had something printed on her cap. Melissa would not have something on her cap—except, it was her. "For crying out loud, could you just turn around so I could see your face?" Almost on cue, she turned around, saw me, and smiled. It was one of the biggest and most memorable smiles I've ever had the privilege of receiving. She was pointing to the top of her cap. I'm usually not this slow on the uptake. What was she pointing to on her cap? That was when it hit me! That was when I realized why she wanted me to be at the ceremony. She wanted me to see that what she had on her cap were the words, "Thanks, Bob!"

The rest of the story is a bit of a blur. I stood there motionless, at least on the outside; my insides were anything but. I instinctively clutched my chest and found myself mouthing the words, "Thank you." It seemed so inadequate, but her nod from across that long, dark hall seemed to indicate that it was exactly right. As I was leaving the ceremony, still in a hurry, but feeling very different from when I arrived, one of Melissa's friends and fellow graduates called out to me, "Quite an honor, eh, Bob?" Yes, I believe you could say that. I believe you could say exactly that.

Well, I'm sad to report that my dad did pass, although not on that day. Melissa went on to achieve great success, not surprisingly, and we're still in contact. Although the years fade our memories, one thing that will not fade is that in my mind, she'll always be my GA and I will always be the one who is thankful.

The Blessing

Kaye Moon Winters

I almost felt guilty sitting at the information station with a shawl wrapped around me for warmth. The hard Texas heat was reflected on the faces of every person entering the building. The frenzy of summer registration had given way to the slow pace of daily campus traffic, and I was contentedly people-watching, looking for someone to assist. Then I saw her—well, him first, actually.

Diminutive though he was, his attire demanded attention: straw cowboy hat, high-heeled boots, and a large belt buckle. He reached out to open the big glass door for her, and her pain preceded her on her path toward me.

I guessed them to be younger than they looked; still, they had some years on them. She was as round as she was tall, and that's not much either way. Her complexion was flushed from the heat. She walked as if she carried an unsteady burden on her back. It caused her to sway. I could see her sighs with each step before I heard them. Barely lifting her stooped shoulders to raise her head, the face she presented to me could serve as a model for an acting class: "Portray weariness."

Our exchange was brief. She hardly met my eyes. "Yes, ma'am, I need to talk to someone about your certified nurse's assistant program." I don't know if it's because, in my capacity as an advisor/recruiter for nontraditional students I'm attuned to their particular needs, but something about her lingered with me. I sent her off in the right direction, but I couldn't shake the sadness she left behind. Not 5 minutes later, someone from the continuing education office across from me came over with a stack of flyers and said, "Kaye, we have some money left in these grants. Would you let students know about these programs?"

"Hmm, what have we got here?" I remember thinking. "Money for welding classes, money for truck driving courses, what's this? CNA? Certified nurse's assistant! Sixteen hundred dollars toward tuition! Where did I send her? Which way did she go?"

I lifted my head in the direction I thought she had taken just in time to see her slowly waddling back. She clutched a bunch of papers in one hand and steadied herself on the arm of her stoic friend with the other. As she met my eyes, something told me to rein in my excitement and approach her like a skittish horse.

"Did you find what you needed?"

"Yes, ma'am. Thank you for your help."

"Well, maybe I can be of further help. Right after you walked away, I got this flyer with information about some grant money that's still available. It's only $1,600, but, that might take some of the worry away."

Her brows furrowed immediately as she took the flyer from my hand. Ever so slowly, I stood and asked, "Do you have time to go over to continuing ed? It's just right over there. That's the office the money is coming out of. They'll be able to guide you through it. Come on, I'll walk you over to the right person."

Four hours later, she and her sidekick were headed out the door, at last. It had been a longer day than either had planned, but they were better for it. When I waved to them, neither could suppress the tiny flame of hope I saw flickering in their tired eyes. Slowly, she made her way over to me. It was the first smile I'd seen, and it revealed more than her missing teeth. "Thank you, ma'am," she whispered. "They said I might get it!"

I am blessed to go home from work just about every day with a sense of fulfillment. This day, for whatever reason, I felt my cup running over. Little did I know that this feeling was just a prelude.

About a week later, I saw her lumbering up to the door, sans her sidekick. From the ready smile she proffered, I was sure she had good news. "Did you get the grant?" I asked, barely containing my excitement. "Well, honey, it looks like I probably won't ..." was all she managed before my cries of dismay drowned her out. "Oh, I'm so sorry! I thought for sure you would ..." and then she interrupted me.

"No, no, don't be disappointed. The blessing is still there. The blessing hasn't been removed. You see, I'm an abuse victim." She had a visceral response to speaking the words aloud. Her hand went to her mouth as it sucked in a great gulp of air. Composing herself, she continued, "My husband beat the teeth out of my head for 25 years. That day you saw me, helped me, well, that was the day my divorce was final, and those were the first steps I'd taken to a new life. I've been driving a truck for all these years because that's what he wanted. I always wanted to be a nurse's assistant, but he said I was too stupid. That grant would be wonderful, but I have the money. I didn't come here needing money. What I needed was somebody like you, somebody to reach out to me and hand me hope. That's what you did. You are the blessing. This school is the blessing."

We both dissolved into tears. I went home that day on a high like I've never known in my professional life.

Soon enough, summer wound down. Finals were over and fall was a short break away. The oppressive heat had lifted, and I didn't feel nearly as guilty sitting there comfortably wrapped in my shawl. After the person I'd been helping moved on, I glanced out to see someone vaguely familiar striding across the parking lot. She took the curb with a jump and fairly bolted through the door. Her smile was blinding, which is good, because I didn't believe my eyes anyway. She was ... transformed! Her walk! Her straight back! *Her joy!* She bounded toward me, came around the desk, and bear-hugged me off the ground. "You're looking at a certified nurse's assistant! Girlfriend, not only did I get that grant, I learned so much and met so many nice people. At first I felt kind of funny, 'cause I was older than everybody else, but I remembered all the things you told me about that and just let it roll off me. The best thing I learned was *I'm not stupid!*"

And the best thing I learned from this? The blessing is in being a student affairs professional. The work I do has the power to change lives, and when this miracle occurs, my life is changed for the better, too. Because of this experience and others like it, I went on to found a support group for nontraditional students on my campus: N2L@SJC. The moniker is an acronym for my favorite George Eliot quote: "It is never too late to be who you might have been." But don't take just my word for it. There's a newly certified CNA in Texas ready to back up the claim.

You Home? Meet Me on the Stairway: Lessons of Living Together

Ryan C. Holmes and Susan D. Longerbeam

D o you want an on-the-ground account of living diversity? Then we hope to inspire you. Our living experience provoked us. It isn't tidy, yet we share our story to stimulate conversations among colleagues about the trials and joys of deepening engagement. So what's new about our story? We—of different races, classes, ages, genders, and sexual orientations—lived in a metropolitan Washington, D.C., home together in a turbulent time (9/11, anthrax, sniper) while enrolled in a student affairs graduate program. The program mission states that it has "an intense focus on multiculturalism and social justice." Could the focus of our program be achieved at home? Because we honestly believed it could, we tried. These letters to each other reflect what we learned over conversations on the stairway. Ours is a story of angst, hope, and love.

DEAR SUSAN,

It has been 6 years since we had a brief introduction at orientation in Maryland—you as a second-year doctoral student, me as a prospective first-year master's student. I did not realize that our lives were about to change forever. When I saw the e-mail from you asking if anyone wanted to share a house, my first thought was, "Well, it might be more economical than finding my own place, but I've never lived with a White chick before." It was easy to navigate the White world for business and in school, but every Black person I know still needs their "time"—time to talk to other Black folks or to cool. I knew I would run the risk of having no outlet, which would, in turn, potentially cause mental harm to me. But then reality set in. The reality that if I found my own spot, since I couldn't afford to work full time, I would not really have the finances or home support to get by. That's when I made the decision to move in.

DEAR RYAN,

As your landlord, I worried that I would continually and unconsciously reveal my White privilege in ugly ways. I worried that I would offend you and, worse, never know it. You see, being White is a lot about the isolation of not knowing my racial self, thus not knowing others, and yearning to connect better. But we fell into this experience—and neither of us was very well prepared. We fell into it because I needed help with the mortgage and you needed help with the rent. So we began, both of us brave in our own way.

Your risk was greater than mine. I risked being revealed as a fake and alienating both you and me. But I learned just what level of risk you were taking at a deeper level when you asked wryly on your second day in Maryland, as we stepped outside the front door to find the bus stop, "Do they still shoot Black men for walking with White women around here?"

Sometimes, I still wonder whether you got the time you needed to be understood and to vent while you lived with me. I appreciate those times you chose to spend with me, particularly when we talked on the stairway, you coming home from a music gig, me just getting up to begin my day. Crossing paths with one another on the stairway was no different than how we had lived our entire lives: coming from dissimilar places and still living in divergent time zones. We met on that stairway often, and gradually we took the conversations to new levels.

DEAR SUSAN,

As a childhood friend and I drove from Louisiana to Maryland, I felt uneasy, anxious, confused, and excited. Though many of these emotions were tied to the new state and school, they were also affected by my future living situation. When I told my friend that you were a White lady, 40 or so, and bisexual, I can still remember his first question: "Man, your mom knows about this?" My reply: "Naw, cuz, I didn't feel like going through that line of questioning." His reply: "Cool." That was it. Though nothing more was said, we realized the dilemma. I was a Black man from Shreveport, whose family roots ran deep in Black/White tension. I was only a stone's throw from the years of Jim Crow and as a Black male, I was not used to being in the same place overnight with White people, let alone living with one. However, I drew strength from the belief that God loves all people and expects us to love each other and get along. Further, I was determined to have an open mind and possessed the will to make anything work, regardless of the initial outlook, especially when all other options did not look favorable.

When we arrived at my new home in Maryland, I remember falling asleep on the floor and being awakened by you. When you came in, I introduced my friend, we exchanged words, and you went up to your room. As soon as you left the room, my friend said the most comforting thing of the day: "I think she's cool; you'll be fine." So our living together began. For months, I did what most southern Black men with any sense would do. I wore the fakest mask I could muster up while observing your spirit. I wanted to see what areas *you* were fake in. Was I a guinea pig to be observed and reported on? Was I only there to make someone White feel good by helping a Black dude who had his back against the wall? Or was this a gift from God, who saw I was trying to make good on my potential and wanted to send me a blessing?

DEAR RYAN,

I went through many emotions in the beginning of our relationship. I struggled with holding a balance of emotions in engaging race: uncertainty, confusion, and guilt, but also openness, interest, happiness, and eagerness. Because you believed in me, you gave me endurance to hold the balance of conflicting emotions and the pain of racism. I struggled with myself over wanting to be helpful but not get in your way. I wanted to welcome you, and I wanted you to feel at home and comfortable. Most of the time, I didn't know what I was doing, but I just kept bumbling through and working on being present. One White colleague said to me that for White folks it is important to be able to sit with the pain and grief of racism. So I sat. You have increased my capacity to sit and listen, and reduced the urgent need to minimize racism.

We lived in D.C. at a time when tensions were high: 9/11 and anthrax hit our region. Just after we moved in, a sniper was killing people near our neighborhood. I will never forget your reaction the morning I heard the news and called down the stairs to tell you they caught the snipers, and they were Black. We were both surprised because most people thought the sniper(s) would be White, given the history of White male serial killers in the United States. You said, "Damn! Why did they have to go and do that? Don't they know we'll all get blamed?"

You had to manage your reputation as a member of a group in ways I did not. You were keenly aware of how you were perceived and how people's perceptions were shaped by their stereotypes. You showed me just how much those stereotypes affected you on a daily basis in a myriad of ways. For example, one day we were talking about getting a dog, and you mentioned that you had always wanted a Rottweiler. I asked why you would want a dog that people were generally afraid of. Your response was an epiphany for me: You said that you could relate to it being that people were afraid for no reason other than how it looked. I learned then that at a deep level you were continually aware of your impact on others.

DEAR SUSAN,

In looking back, there were many light-hearted times and funny situations. Once, you wanted to help me make collard greens, substituting salt pork with olive oil. The first excuse I could come up with to make you leave the greens at the grocery was that they looked unhealthy. This situation gave me new insight about us, in that I thought I had been clever enough to come up with an excuse that didn't hurt your feelings. However, you knew what I was doing all along and chose to laugh about your "California hippie cooking."

I also recall the many conversations we had at home. They covered race, religion, sexuality, and politics. Engaging these topics would not allow our relationship to be shallow and made us both realize that we wanted truth over political correctness. For instance, I realized you knew that gay relationships made me uncomfortable. Let's face it, I was a recovering homophobe. In the neighborhood where I grew up, the worst thing was to be gay. Many fights were started as a consequence of being labeled gay. As a result of these experiences, as well as my religious up-bringing, in which preachers spoke of being gay as the worst sin, opportunities to process my feelings on the subject were rare. Instead of letting it go and acting as if no problem was present, you chose to challenge me every time an opportunity presented itself. Nonetheless, when you challenged, you did so kindly.

Who would ever have thought I would grow to like tofu? Start to read the nutrition information on boxes? Be able to say that I am not homophobic—and mean it—and not care what someone else might say? Find a White person who actually cared about me as only a family member could? Tell myself it's okay not to be as hard as the world was making me while continuing to understand that I have to work twice as hard to achieve, regardless of how unfair it may seem? Thanks.

DEAR RYAN,

Some of my best memories are the sounds of you filling the house with song, and your lessons about music are forever with me. But the greatest lessons came from taking the risk to let go of my defenses. The support of your friendship encouraged me to show you my underbelly.

Remember that time you said "Euww" when two men kissed on TV? My heart sank with the familiar feeling of being completely rejected. I slowly walked upstairs to think. A few days later I chose to speak with you about sexual orientation. I consciously chose to trust you, to take a risk on behalf of our friendship. You came through when you brought up the topic of sexual orientation the second time, without any effort from me. I remember my eyes tearing up, and that's when I knew we would be alright. That's when I knew the depth of your integrity, your commitment to examine your thoughts, and your brilliance to open yourself up to your own knowledge. I learned that I could express the most vulnerable parts of me, especially those about my gender and my sexual orientation, and you would have a heart and mind that were big enough to embrace me and open enough to reconsider your own thinking. Because you showed me your openness about homophobia, you renewed my hope that I could travel through the world as authentically me. Hope about homophobia has been a rare experience in my life.

DEAR SUSAN,

There are other conflicts between us that are important to mention, specifically the times I struggled in our early relationship. I can remember that you would hear negative things about me and still you would want to protect me. The criticism was often of my world view as someone from a marginalized group. You would always ask, "What do you want me to tell 'em?" "What should I do?" Though I admired your feelings of support, I also was perturbed by them. I am a fighter by nature and circumstance, a fighter who must remain strong and continue to have sharpened skills to navigate life. I felt coddled, and although you were caring, I hadn't felt that sort of caring since before high school. I thought you didn't know the difference between babying and supporting. I had to readjust my idea of what it meant to be cared for.

DEAR RYAN,

I am sorry for those times I coddled you. I imagine the coddling was worse because I am White. I struggle with my Whiteness in terms of wanting to make amends. Though I understand I am not responsible for racial inequities, I want to live my life in ways that hold me responsible for creating a just future. As in so much between us, there were complexities of difference operating. I think there was a gender dynamic, in that I wanted to protect you in a feminine way. Fiercely loyal, I struggle with wanting to protect loved ones.

With loved ones, we sometimes need to give them room. What made our challenge more difficult is that we were living with each other. As you mentioned, we didn't have "down time." If I had challenged your homophobia, our home could have fallen apart. If you had challenged my privileged coddling, it could have fallen apart as well. But we made it through. Because we are bound to the truth, we are both stronger people, and so is our friendship.

DEAR SUSAN,

Once you didn't care for a friend of mine. I saw through him, and understood his heart. He was wearing a mask like many do, the mask that one has to wear at times when they are different from societal norms. You saw him when he felt comfortable enough to remove his mask and be himself. When you told me you didn't like him, it was the first time I heard you say that about anybody. I wondered why you would feel that way. How could you be the same person who could find the good in anyone, and not understand he had been shaped by his environment as I had been by mine? I had to ask myself, "I wonder if she feels this way because he's White?" Sometimes I wondered if you were harder on White people than those of other races. I thought you dualistically criticized Whites while giving Blacks the benefit of the doubt. Over time, you started to see who he was and became more open-minded about his behavior because you could see his heart. Thanks for being the champion I knew you to be.

DEAR RYAN,

I'm having a familiar reaction to you—the realization that you see through me, and I cannot hide. Yes, I have been more critical of White people—criticism is a part of my discomfort with my own Whiteness that I project onto others. Thank you for being patient with me as I continue to work through my weaknesses.

DEAR SUSAN,

These letters cannot begin to discuss everything we have meant to each other. The fact is, we both learned more by sitting at home together, figuring out what makes each other great, secretly vowing to do the best we could to make sure the other was comfortable, and all the time challenging each other to be better for others and ourselves. I can say that of all the classes I've taken that focused on diversity, society, social skills, and counseling, I learned more at home with my roommate. I wonder how much can be learned in a structured residential community for undergraduate students, especially as the education we offered each other could never be presented in a class. I love you not just for who you are, but for everything you aided me in becoming. I look at the fact that so many of our personal characteristics differed, yet still we shared the view that seeing the humanity in another trumps all else. Thanks for being a friend and for struggling with me when others may not have been in a position to see my pain. Likewise, I am grateful that you chose to celebrate my promise rather than highlight my problems and that you chose to learn from me instead of seeing my ways as an alternative. Our interactions are what friendships long to be, what we wish college courses could cover. They hold the truth to help the United States become the country it can be if we actualize the potential of our multiculturalism.

DEAR RYAN,

You bridged many divides for me. So much of my identity of race and sexual orientation has been about trying to bridge, to regain lost humanity, to overcome alienation. At times, I've been lonely. Our ability to connect with each other heals me. Friendship across differences isn't easy, and it requires honesty. I'm able to love you better because you've had the courage and the intellectual rigor required to tell me the truth. You've told me that you don't like being shielded. You don't like me being inconsistent, being closed, being hardest on other White people. I've shown you I like nonviolence and I don't like homophobia. We improve each other.

My learning, too, has been deeper and more visceral than any I would have experienced in a classroom. When I reflect on our living together, what I appreciate most is your presence. You have a loving spirit. The joy you brought into our living situation was palpable. I reflect on your presence sometimes in the tough times, when I work with race and power and privilege. Those times are always chosen, because in my Whiteness, I have the privilege to choose not to address these topics, even in the courses I teach. Thank you for contributing to my journey in a way that helps me remain positive and feel renewed. I treasure our friendship and want to offer hope for others on the challenging and rewarding journey of honesty across differences.

SUMMARY OF OUR LEARNING

Ryan, as a result of our shared living, I'm now more at ease with my Whiteness, my privilege, and my bisexuality—and discussing these identities with other people. I have the ease of not defending the dynamics of racism and privilege, and I usually recognize them, even when they are relatively subtle. For example, yesterday I used a restaurant's bathroom without purchasing anything and verbalized my use of privilege to my partner. You helped me learn ease with my Whiteness. I have more fun and I experience more joy in multicultural settings. I've learned to share my mistakes more openly, hopefully to the benefit of students. I think about race with more relativism, and I am less quick to judge other White people and am more honest with people of color. Taking responsibility for race gives my life and my teaching purpose and meaning. I reflect on the lessons you taught me on the stairway. Your teaching sustains me.

Susan, as a result of our relationship, I can better see how leaving issues undiscussed can hinder us as individuals and as a society. I have grown to understand that if anyone has a view not endorsed by the mainstream, most times it takes someone from a position of power (e.g., straight, White) to shed light on issues for them to lend an ear—simply because those in power are more palatable. Additionally, I am encouraged to speak up even more for myself in all situations. Though I have never been a shy person when it comes to offering my views, I had to come to grips with the fact that in "mixed company" I would sometimes reserve my opinions to maintain peace. Though I still believe there is a time and place for everything, I also believe that it is senseless for anyone to swallow discomfort while others fail to realize the environments they create. Furthermore, I am able to recognize the ways in which my identity holds power. Because I am male and straight, there are situations in which I am given an unearned advantage. Finally, I realize the importance of just *being* and allowing others to do the same. I have less of a need to compartmentalize and label people. As I continue to stretch myself, there are parts of the authentic me that survive. As I wish personal freedom for others, I am reminded of you—who showed me that a person is only as free as she wishes to be. Thanks for being a living example on the stairway, of taking the risk to engage our differences.

Boxers On...Fire Alarms Off!

Vicki L. McNeil

Often during midterms or finals, students living in the residence halls would pull a fire alarm and unload one of the freshmen residence halls. On this particular fall evening, a freshman male returned to the halls extremely intoxicated. He went to his room but reappeared later still intoxicated and only wearing his boxers. He pulled his floor fire alarm and at the same time pulled off his boxers and dropped them below the alarm on the floor.

Anytime a fire alarm goes off, every student must evacuate the building. As the resident assistants shepparded students down the stairs and outside, along came the student who pulled the fire alarm. He was buck-naked and seemed quite nonchalant. He walked around chatting with students—hanging out figuratively and literally. College students never seem to let anything faze them. No one took issue with his nakedness and his nudity certainly didn't keep them from talking to him.

However, one of the resident directors did notice his lack of clothing and confronted him. He told the student, "Get some clothes on right now!" The student just stood there with a glazed look and said to the RD (resident director), "I don't have any clothes cause I dropped my boxers on the ground next to the fire alarm when I pulled the alarm." The resident director immediately grabbed the student by the arm, pulled him into the housing office and gave him a towel to wear for the duration of the fire alarm evacuation.

I had the questionable pleasure of dealing with this student in a student judicial hearing. Thank goodness for me, he was fully clothed the day of the hearing, but his memory was a little weak on the details. Memory always seems to evade a student when confronted with the facts and when alcohol is part of the equation.

CONTRIBUTING AUTHORS

MATTHEW BIRNBAUM is a professor of higher education and student affairs at the University of Northern Colorado. He earned a PhD and MA from the Center for the Study of Higher Education at the University of Arizona. Prior to becoming a faculty member, Matt spent 15 years working as a student affairs administrator.

SCOTT C. BROWN currently serves as associate vice president and dean of students at Colgate University. Previously, he was director of the Daniel L. Jones Career Development Center at Mount Holyoke College. He served as the chair of the 2005 American College Personnel Association (ACPA) National Convention; was an editorial member of the *Journal of College Student Development;* and received the Fulbright Seminar Grant (Germany), ACPA *Annuit Coeptis* (New Professionals), and the ACPA Emerging Scholar awards.

STAN CARPENTER is professor and chair of the Educational Administration and Psychological Services Department at Texas State University–San Marcos. He earned a BS in mathematics from Tarleton State University, an MS in student personnel and guidance from Texas A&M–Commerce, and a PhD in counseling and student personnel services from the University of Georgia. He has served as the executive director of the Association for the Study of Higher Education (ASHE) and as editor/chair of the ACPA media board, as well as the National Association of Student Personnel Administrators (NASPA) board of directors.

DORIS CHING served as vice president for student affairs at the University of Hawaii from 1987 until her retirement in 2005. She received an EdD from Arizona State University and a BEd and MEd from the University of Hawaii. Doris was the first woman of color and first Asian/Pacific Islander to be elected president of NASPA and the NASPA Foundation.

LES COOK currently serves as the vice president for student affairs at Michigan Technological University. He has held positions at a variety of institutions, including the University of Utah, University of the Pacific, Salt Lake Community College, and the University of Nebraska. Les has a doctorate of education in educational leadership from Brigham Young University. He began a 2-year term in spring 2009 as regional vice president for NASPA IV–East.

JACQUELINE COOPER holds a bachelor's degree in mass communications and a master of science degree in education from Jackson State University. She received her PhD in higher education administration from the University of Missouri, where she was a Thurgood Marshall and Velma Deuce Fellow. Currently, she is an assistant professor of student affairs at Texas State University–San Marcos.

MICHELE ASHA COOPER is president of the Institute for Higher Education Policy. She received her BA from the College of Charleston, an MPS from Cornell University, and a PhD from the University of Maryland, College Park.

CHERYL DALY is an assistant professor and director of the College Student Personnel Program at Western Carolina University. Her research interests focus on ways to improve the work environment for diverse faculty and the learning environment for diverse students. In particular, Cheryl examines the ways that organizational structures and cultures shape both faculty roles and teaching/learning contexts.

KATHLEEN LIS DEAN is assistant vice president for assessment and planning in student affairs at John Carroll University. She earned her PhD in education policy and leadership at the University of Maryland, College Park; her MEd in student personnel administration/college counseling from the University of Delaware; and her BA in international relations from the University of Delaware.

DAVID DIELSI has taught and tutored students in mathematics at community colleges, small private colleges, and large state universities for more than 20 years. He holds degrees in chemical engineering and mathematics education. Currently, he works in the Upward Bound program at the University of Vermont in Burlington.

ANNE EHRLICH is the dean of students at Woodbury University. She received her bachelor's degree in psychology from the University of California, San Diego; her master's degree in social work from the University of Michigan; and her doctorate in educational leadership from the University of California, Los Angeles.

LINDA GILLINGHAM is the assistant director of undergraduate academic services/coordinator of graduation auditing and advising at Central Michigan University. Prior to her career in advising, she taught music at the elementary, middle school, and college levels. She currently is an adjunct instructor of music education at Central Michigan University and has been a full-time advisor for the past 15 years.

CHRISTOPHER L. HADDIX graduated from Michigan Technological University in December 2008 with a bachelor of science degree in applied ecology and environmental science. He is currently working on a research project with a faculty member in forest resources and environmental sciences. Upon completion of his research project, Chris aspires to find employment in the field of environmental science and pursue an honorable and rewarding life.

JAMES D. HARDWICK serves as vice president for student life at Carroll College in Helena, Montana. He has a doctorate of education in educational policy and administration from the University of Minnesota; a master of education in counselor education from North Dakota State University; and a bachelor of science from Minnesota State University Moorhead, with a double major in management and political science.

APRIL K. HEISELT is an assistant professor in the Department of Counseling and Educational Psychology at Mississippi State University. She received her PhD in educational leadership and policy and an MPA from the University of Utah. Her teaching emphasis is in student affairs in higher education, and her primary research interest explores the impact of civic engagement on student and faculty learning.

JOY HOFFMAN has worked in higher education for almost 15 years. Her experience includes orientation, student activities, student government, sexual violence prevention programs, and multicultural services. She currently serves as the director of the cultural center at Whittier College and is a second-year doctoral student at California Lutheran University.

RYAN C. HOLMES is the director of off-campus communities for LaSalle University. He has master's degrees from the University of Maryland in college student personnel and from La Salle University in bilingual/bicultural studies. Ryan is a certified mediator with the ASJA Gehring Institute, and trains resident and community assistants in conflict mediation.

JOHN M. HOWE is a doctoral student in higher education and student affairs at Indiana University in Bloomington. His interest in international student affairs stems from previous experiences teaching in Taiwan, the United Arab Emirates, India, and Afghanistan.

ROBYN HUDSON is an assistant director in Services for Students with Disabilities at Virginia Tech. Robyn is a licensed clinical social worker in Virginia and holds an MSW from Radford University. Currently, she is pursuing a PhD in curriculum and instruction from Virginia Tech.

RAYNA A. ISAKI graduated from the University of Hawaii at Manoa (UHM) in May 2007 with a BA in psychology and a minor in sociology. She is currently at UHM in the educational administration program, focusing on higher education.

MARCIA KENNARD KIESSLING serves as assistant vice chancellor of student activities, diversity, and special projects at the University of North Carolina at Charlotte. Marcia received her undergraduate degree from the University of Evansville in Indiana and her master's degree from Western Illinois University. She is currently working on her doctorate at North Carolina State University. Marcia also serves as NASPA Region III public policy coordinator.

LINDA M. LEMIESZ received her PhD in comparative literature from Columbia University and her JD from New York Law School. Since 1992, she has served as dean of students at the Cooper Union for the Advancement of Science and Art.

SUSAN D. LONGERBEAM is an assistant professor and coordinator of the student affairs preparation program at Northern Arizona University. She has a master's degree in health services administration from Antioch University and a PhD from the University of Maryland in college student personnel.

SAMUEL R. LOPEZ JR. is a second-year master's candidate in the college student affairs program at Pennsylvania State University. He earned his bachelor's degree in deviant behavior and social control at John Jay College of Criminal Justice, New York.

CAROL A. LUNDBERG teaches in college counseling and student development at Azusa Pacific University. She has a BA in social ecology from the University of California, Irvine; an MA in student development from Azusa Pacific University; and a PhD in higher education from Claremont Graduate University.

SARAH M. MARSHALL is an assistant professor of educational leadership and director of doctoral programs at Central Michigan University. She earned her PhD and MA from Loyola University Chicago. Prior to becoming a faculty member, Sarah spent 8 years working as a student affairs administrator. She edited the first volume of *Stories of Inspiration: Lessons and Laughter in Student Affairs*.

VICKI L. MCNEIL is vice president of student affairs at Armstrong Atlantic State University in Savannah, Georgia. She has a bachelor's in music education; a master of science in curriculum and instruction; and a doctor of education in student personnel administration from Oklahoma State University. She has more than 27 years of experience in student affairs work at the University of Oklahoma, Temple University, Loyola University New Orleans, and Armstrong Atlantic State University.

LYNETTE S. MERRIMAN is the senior associate dean for student affairs at the University of Southern California (USC). She earned an EdD in educational leadership and an MA in higher education and from the University of California, Los Angeles, and holds a BA in journalism from USC.

ELIZABETH M. MILLER is currently an area coordinator of residential education at California State University, San Bernardino. She obtained her BA in communication studies and an MS in counseling and student development in higher education from California State University, Long Beach.

KAYE MOON WINTERS is affiliated with the Texas Association of College Admission Counseling (TACAC). She works at San Jacinto College Central in Pasadena, Texas, as an advisor/recruiter for nontraditional students and is the founder of N2L@SJC, a support group for nontraditional students. She received her AA from San Jacinto College in 2005 and was a 60-year-old summa cum laude graduate of the University of Houston in 2007. Her BA was in English/creative writing.

MICHELE C. MURRAY is the assistant vice president for student development at Seattle University. She received her PhD in education policy and leadership from the University of Maryland, her master's degree in higher education and student affairs administration from the University of Vermont, and her bachelor's degree in psychology and rhetoric & communication studies from the University of Virginia.

JENNIFER O'CONNOR is a faculty member in the higher education program at Suffolk University in Boston, Massachusetts. She received her undergraduate degree from Amherst College and her master's and doctoral degrees from Boston College. Her research and publications focus on social class equity in higher education.

BOB ORRANGE has been the associate director of the University at Buffalo (UB) career services office since 1999 and in student affairs in the State University of New York (SUNY) system since 1989. He has graduate degrees in both English and college student personnel administration and an undergraduate degree in communications. In addition, Bob has written three children's books and is a frequent speaker at conferences and workshops.

NATALIE PAGEL received her undergraduate degree in English and French from Oklahoma State University in 2004. Currently, she is working toward a master's degree in adult and higher education with an emphasis in student affairs at the University of Oklahoma. She co-advises the housing center student administration.

TY PATTERSON is the part-time director of the Center of Excellence for Tobacco-Free Campus Policy at Ozarks Technical Community (OTC) college. In 2008, he retired as vice president of student services at OTC. He received the Missouri ACPA Lifetime Achievement Award named in honor of Dr. Richard Capel in 2006.

KRISTINE A. PETERSON is currently pursuing her master's in student affairs administration at Michigan State University (MSU) and will graduate in May 2009. She also serves as an assistant hall director at MSU. She received her bachelor of science degree in public relations and writing from Northern Michigan University.

GEORGIA PULLEN is the dean of student services at the North Dakota State College of Science (NDSCS) in Wahpeton. Georgia earned an MS in administration from Central Michigan University and a BS in professional and organizational communications from the University of the State of New York.

KRISTEN RENN is associate professor of higher, adult, and lifelong education at Michigan State University. She worked as a student affairs professional for 10 years before earning her PhD and becoming a faculty member. Her research includes the National Study of New Professionals in Student Affairs, a project on LGBT student leaders, and an international study of women's colleges and universities.

PENNY RICE has been the director of the Margaret Sloss Women's Center at Iowa State University since October 2000. Penny returned to college as a single mother with two small children and earned her BS in psychology/women's studies and her MS in counseling and student personnel from Minnesota State University, Mankato. She will complete her doctoral degree in educational leadership and policy studies in May 2009.

SHEILA BUSTILLOS REYNOLDS is a member of the Texas Association of College University Student Personnel Administrators (TACUSPA), where she has served as the graduate student caucus chair. Using her experience as a college athlete, she is coaching the Texas state women's club volleyball team, which is currently ranked 13th in the nation.

HEATHER T. ROWAN-KENYON is an assistant professor of higher education at the University of Virginia. She is the coordinator of the student affairs practice in higher education master's program. Heather earned her PhD in higher education policy and leadership at the University of Maryland, an MA in college student personnel at Bowling Green

State University, and a BS in secondary education/social studies at the University of Scranton.

RONNI SANLO is the program director of the MEd in student affairs at UCLA and the director of the UCLA LGBT Center. Ronni earned both a master's and doctorate in education from the University of North Florida in Jacksonville. She is an active member of NASPA and currently sits on the NASPA board as the Professional Standards chair.

RISHI SRIRAM serves as assistant dean for student learning and engagement at Baylor University. In his current role, he works with living–learning programs, faculty in residence, and research concerning student success.

KENNETH L. STONER is assistant vice chancellor for student affairs and executive director of university housing at the University of Tennessee in Knoxville. He received a BS in physical sciences from Kansas State University, an MS in college student personnel from Iowa State University, and an EdD in educational administration from the University of Tennessee.

MEGAN A. STONE is in her second year of graduate school at Ohio University, where she is pursuing a master's degree in college student personnel. Her graduate assistantship is with the office of the vice president for student affairs, where her primary focus is on the graduate assistant selection process. Megan graduated magna cum laude with a bachelor of science degree in both psychology and health and physical education from Virginia Tech.

LAURA THOMPSON is the assistant dean of students at Franklin College Switzerland. She holds a master's degree in counseling and educational psychology with an emphasis in college student development from the University of Nevada, Reno, and a bachelor's degree in communication studies from the University of San Diego. She has worked in student affairs since 1994 and has lived internationally for the past 6 years.

LEE BURDETTE WILLIAMS is vice president and dean of students at Wheaton College. She has been a department editor of, and frequent contributor to, *About Campus* and is a consultant and speaker with an interest in learning communities and student culture. Lee received her PhD in college student personnel administration from the University of Maryland, College Park, in 1992.

"LEAF" YI ZHANG was born and raised in Zhengzhou, China, and received bachelor's degrees from Zhengzhou University and Fort Hays State University. She earned a master's in communication studies from Fort Hays State University and is currently pursuing a PhD in educational leadership and policy studies at Iowa State University.